The Social Media Imperative

The Social Media Imperative

*School Leadership and Strategies
for Success*

Second Edition

Kristin Magette

NSRA National School Public Relations Association

ROWMAN & LITTLEFIELD
Lanham • Boulder • New York • London

Published by Rowman & Littlefield
A wholly owned subsidiary of The Rowman & Littlefield Publishing Group, Inc.
4501 Forbes Boulevard, Suite 200, Lanham, Maryland 20706
www.rowman.com

Unit A, Whitacre Mews, 26-34 Stannary Street, London SE11 4AB

British Library Cataloguing in Publication Information Available

Library of Congress Cataloging-in-Publication Data Is Available

ISBN 978-1-4758-4196-1 (cloth: alk. paper)
ISBN 978-1-4758-4197-8 (pbk: alk. paper)
ISBN 978-1-4758-4198-5 (electronic)

∞ ™ The paper used in this publication meets the minimum requirements of American National Standard for Information Sciences Permanence of Paper for Printed Library Materials, ANSI/NISO Z39.48-1992.

Printed in the United States of America

To Matthew, Rachel, and each student in our schools. You deserve every last drop of opportunity that the digital world offers. This book is for you.

Contents

Foreword

In the past five years, social media has exploded everywhere. At the National School Public Relations Association, when we complete communication audits for school districts, we see examples where social media is part of the communication strategy for the school community— rather than just an occasional posting or two. Some use social media without ever establishing a clear purpose for their efforts, but where it is effective, it has become a strategic program, rather than just another tool.

In this second edition, Kristin Magette gives you a relevant playbook to develop a purposeful, comprehensive program and helps you decide just how far you want to go in building a tailored program that meets your district's needs and community's wishes. She offers numerous practical examples to save you time and effort. Her insight gives you "next-step" solutions to potential barriers, whether you are just starting or are ready to enhance your social media communications program.

And so much has changed since her first edition, published in 2014. Kristin mentioned to me that when she wrote the first edition, she had difficulty finding a principal or teacher to use as a role model. By contrast, the challenge writing this edition was narrowing down the role models to highlight from the hundreds and thousands that now exist in education, district to district and classroom to classroom.

Just a few of the practical features of this book:

- Updated board policy that is truly focused on allowing social media into schools and encouraging employees to use it for communication, teaching, and learning.
- Tips to monitor and influence conversations that are taking place outside your official channels, including closed and private groups where naysayers may gather to express frustration and spread rumors.
- Opportunities offered by live video, which didn't even exist when the first edition was published. This edition includes practical tips for its successful use, as well as compelling examples from her work and other districts.
- Strategies for leaders, especially superintendents, on using social media with intent—and the support of your school board.

- Examples of handbook policies and community guidelines that outline expectations for appropriate use of social media by employees,
  students, and even parents and community members.

Social media gives you a powerful opportunity to build trust and
become a go-to resource for truth-telling in your community. As we all
know, today anyone with an opinion can post and spread their own
"brand" of what is allegedly happening in your schools. When you establish a credible voice on social media, you build trust with the people
across your school community, through good times and bad. This book
shows you how.

Not only is this edition a must-read contribution to our field of school
communication, but it's also an easy and quick read, providing easy-to-
find help on the situations you face while challenging you to do more
with a purposeful benefit for your schools. And the best part is, Kristin's
solutions have been tested through her work and by NSPRA colleagues
throughout North America.

Kristin Magette has done it again. Heed her advice, and your social
media program will be better tomorrow than it is today.

—Rich Bagin, APR, executive director, National School Public Relations
Association

Preface

In late 2011, I was a thirty-something communications director working for a fifty-something superintendent. In my personal life I wasn't necessarily social media obsessed, but I very much enjoyed living my life in the world of social sharing.

Now and then, I would talk to a teacher in my district—sometimes including my high school science teacher husband—excited about a project they'd seen or thought of that used social media in the classroom. Some had ideas for an interactive blog, others for Facebook pages or groups. A friend who advised the high school student newspaper was looking at ways to share her students' work in the community, particularly since the closing of our hometown paper the year prior.

As I heard these ideas and had these conversations, I would file them away, certain that I would formulate a proposal at some point to help teachers embrace social media in their work—or, at the very least, propose filter changes to allow teachers to access these types of sites on the district network. And in the meantime, I would continue to maintain our district's Facebook page, exploring its potential for reaching our families and other stakeholder groups—and using some of the more successful posts as illustration to help my social-media-non-savvy superintendent, Don Grosdidier, get more comfortable with the world of social media.

A few months later, Don had just come back from a meeting with other superintendents from the region where he had heard a presentation on social media in schools and about all the opportunities available to reach and teach kids. He casually called me into his office, mentioned the meeting, and began asking me a few questions about what he'd heard. I could tell he was intrigued. Then he asked me to tell him why we should be afraid. "Tell me every risk you can think of," he said. "What all could go wrong?"

After listening to me rattle off the dozen or so negative or scary things I could think of on the spot, he paused. He was thinking. And then he said something I will never forget.

"We need to think about these risks," he began. "But we can't stop there because *the opportunities are bigger than the risks*. If we can figure out a way to overcome the fears and mitigate the risks, we won't have to put our heads in the sand and shut this out of our schools. We can leverage the opportunities for social media.

"*Kristin,*" he said. "*This is basic risk management.*"

This moment of realization changed our entire thinking about social media in Eudora Schools. It changed Don's comfort level about embracing something he didn't fully know himself. And it changed my understanding of how leaders discern a move into the relative unknown.

For the first time I realized: If a leader can see a social media embrace through the risk management lens, direct personal knowledge or experience isn't essential. These same leaders put kids on buses and let first graders go out to recess. They hire cafeteria employees who handle hot equipment and serve food to thousands of people each day. They support the need for wood shop and auto repair classes. They allow specialists to work on roofs and make electrical repairs. Personal experience or not, risk management gives leaders the protection and confidence to allow these things to take place in schools each and every day.

As we began our work, Don named the three components of risk management that would allow us to safely embrace social media in our schools: policy, procedures, and professional development. And in the years since—working in Eudora and advising dozens of school districts of all sizes across North America—I've learned that his instinct was exactly right.

Embracing social media isn't scary or complicated. It is, in fact, very simple. And most importantly, it is full of opportunity. In this book, we will examine the three Ps—key strategies for managing risk for social media. We also will explore specific ways to build the trust, consensus, and momentum needed to bring everyone—leaders, teachers, parents, students—along on this journey. The world has changed, and the time for education leaders and school systems everywhere to embrace this social shift is now.

Acknowledgments

Quite simply, this book would not have been possible without:

My friends on #k12PRchat and from the National School Public Relations Association, who inspire me every single day. Thank you for your generous sharing, support, encouragement—and abundant GIFs—as we carve out best practices for social media in schools. Words cannot adequately express my gratitude for this smart, creative, fearless, and loyal tribe.

My now-retired superintendent, Don Grosdidier, who trusted that social media could provide exciting opportunities to our teachers and students—and who pinpointed the simple genius that embracing social media is basic risk management. And Ben Smith, the social media strategist and gifted entrepreneur who served as our guide and advisor as we built the systems to manage risk and leverage opportunity. The lasting influence of these two collaborative leaders can be found on virtually every page of this book.

The entire Eudora Schools family: administrators who harness the power of social media for engagement, school board members who see the big picture, families and friends who make our social media communities great, and most especially the teachers who every day show the incredible things that can happen when social media is placed in expert hands as a tool for teaching and learning. It is my honor and privilege to share their stories in this book. My thanks also go to Eudora superintendent Steve Splichal, who has graciously allowed me to support other school districts' social media work with this book and other endeavors.

And finally, my husband Eric—my favorite teacher who can articulate what digital learners deserve and how systems can evolve to make that possible. You are my fact checker, my idea bouncer and collaborator, and my continual reminder that teachers are a school district's greatest asset. And you are the husband and father who has, once again, supported all the phases of crazy that come when I say "yes" to another project. Thank you.

Introduction

Social media has forever changed the people in our schools—our students, our families, and our employees. But have our schools adapted to take advantage of the opportunities this change represents? Now is the time for education leaders to confront this conflict and create the potential for each school system to be an active and engaging part of the digital world.

The journey begins with a compelling case for why social media is critical to twenty-first-century learning environments. But simply understanding *why* it's important won't persuade those who are most anxious about social media's landmines. It's essential to examine the legitimate risks and fears about social media that exist within all school communities. It is only by understanding and appreciating these dangers—sometimes real, sometimes exaggerated—that buy-in can be achieved among those decision makers critical to system change.

This book will explain how to use a collaborative process to design board policies, procedures, and professional development programs in a way that engages and reassures stakeholders. These three indispensable elements make up the foundation of a social media embrace by acknowledging opportunities, outlining expectations and consequences, and supporting all those who work in the school system.

Once the social media shift has begun, employees at all levels can begin to enjoy the powerful advantages that social media provides, with the knowledge and guidelines to make professional, safe, and positive decisions. Social media opportunities for professional development, student instruction, communication, and crisis management all will be explored.

Throughout this book, readers will learn specific steps to take to frame a social media embrace in terms of risk management—mitigating risk to enjoy the very real opportunities provided to educators and leaders in the digital world of social media.

ONE

Social Media Matters to Schools

It's 8 a.m. on a Thursday in a nearby school parking lot. Parents and buses are dropping off kids near the front doors of the school. Teenagers are parking their cars and wandering toward the front doors. Thirty minutes ago, teachers, principals, office professionals, paraeducators, and others were arriving on campus and making preparations to begin the day.

Although the morning school arrival routine changes very little from one generation to the next, when you sit and watch these events unfold in the parking lot each morning, there is one thing you'll see that you would not have seen only a few years ago: People are using technology to connect with the world and document their day. From their smartphones, adults are checking their calendar for the day, glancing at their email inbox, or making a call to confirm a dentist appointment for the afternoon. Teenagers are texting with friends, trying to figure out a new game, or listening to a favorite playlist.

And in that same school parking lot, nearly everyone is watching life unfold on social media. They're seeing updates from friends and family. They're reading news about last night's PTO meeting, details about the early morning fire truck sirens they heard, or the latest updates on everyone from Kim Kardashian to Kim Jong-un. In countless ways, our families' everyday lives are taking place on a small device kept in a purse, pocket, or backpack.

There's no question: Our world is digital. Whether students or employees, the community of people who make up our schools are living an ever-increasing part of their lives online. And if we ask them to unplug from this real-time, dynamic, content-rich digital world when they walk through the doors of our school, we miss out. Big-time. We miss opportunities to communicate quickly and directly. We miss opportunities to

1

teach and learn. We miss opportunities to build relationships and create trust through transparency. And we miss opportunities to better connect to the community in and around our school.

In 2013, Eudora School District leaders resolved to *stop missing these opportunities*. Through a collaborative process focused on policy, procedures, and professional development, the work began toward a district-wide embrace of the social media shift. Choices were made to stop shutting this new world out of schools and to begin harnessing its power for the entire school community. This work can be done in any district, large or small, rich or poor. And the time is now.

OUR "CONSTANTLY CONNECTED" WORLD

In 2014, Nielsen's Digital Consumer Report characterized just how dramatically Americans' lives are shifting into the digital world.[1]

> The number of digital devices and platforms available to today's consumers has exploded in recent years. As a result, today's consumer is more connected than ever, with more access to and deeper engagement with content and brands. And these changes are contributing to the media revolution and blurring traditional media definitions.
>
> Americans now own four digital devices on average, and the average U.S. consumer spends 60 hours a week consuming content across devices. And a majority of U.S. households now own high-definition televisions (HDTVs), Internet-connected computers and smartphones. In addition to more devices, consumers also have more choices for how and when they access content.
>
> As a result, consumption habits are changing. [. . .] And social media usage is now standard practice in our daily lives—almost half (47%) of smartphone owners visit social networks every day.
>
> It has never been a more important time to know how consumers are behaving than in today's fast-evolving digital environment. These trends in digital technology are propelling consumers' new multi-screen, constantly connected lifestyles.

In 2017, Nielsen released a report showing that social media use has continued to increase, especially in the demographic groups that represent our school districts' parents, particularly mothers, and the trend reaches across cultural groups. Furthermore, the report showed that the percentage of time spent by adults on social media continues to increase, 34 percent or more since the end of 2015.[2]

Social media no doubt introduces challenges in our schools, but the data is clear that the reliance on digital and mobile technologies by those in our school community can no longer be ignored. The world is changing, and expectations are shifting. Schools and districts must adapt to this shift if we intend to remain relevant and influential to our students and families, and in our communities.

BRING THE DIGITAL WORLD INTO THE CLASSROOM

Picture again the school parking lot, with students arriving for the day and walking into school. Now, imagine what it means when we require that they check their digital world at the door before entering our world of classrooms. Will they be motivated and engaged? Will learning feel meaningful and relevant? Will they find school to be a place that challenges them to grow? Or will school become a more and more artificial environment that is less and less connected to their real life outside of school?

As education leaders, we can't afford to let our schools be a place that isn't connected to real life. For decades, schools have succeeded because educators have dedicated themselves to creating schools that reflect the communities where they are built. Throughout history, schools have adapted along the economic and cultural trends of agriculture, industry, and a wide range of changing social norms. The digital world and social media are the new shifts that require adaptation, and the time has come for education leaders who believe in embracing students and preparing them for a bright future to understand this reality and its implications.

The shift toward social media and digital technology didn't happen overnight, even if the pace of change makes it feel like it did! And this constant and rapid change certainly brings with it a host of legitimate concerns and fears. But the best education leaders—board members, district and building administrators, teacher leaders—are deeply and personally vested in the quality of the educational environment where they work. Surely it's incumbent on anyone who cares this deeply to proceed both mindfully and cautiously, but to proceed nonetheless. We can no longer responsibly choose to ignore this shift. We must embrace it—our learning communities depend on it.

No longer is the question whether the world where we live and teach is digital—there can be no doubt that it is. The question education leaders must now ask is this: Are we helping our students become good digital citizens in this digital world? School systems rely on policy, internet filters, and school rules to manage the many concerns associated with technology tools. These are critical elements of operating a safe, supportive school for students and staff.

The problem comes, however, when the policies, filters, and rules shut out the digital world to a point where students are no longer able to genuinely engage with the best learning. By removing access to all social media at school, education leaders miss out on a tremendous opportunity to teach students how to use social media tools constructively, how to use them for learning.

Blocking social networks does nothing to help us mentor tweens and teens to use social media wisely so the doors will stay open as they seek college and career pathways after graduation. And eliminating such social networks as Facebook, Twitter, Instagram, and others from teachers' toolboxes cuts down on the ways they can engage students on a highly relevant, highly motivating level. We can do better.

Without question, there are very real risks and challenges associated with using social media in schools, and we will explore those in chapter 2. But the greatest risk today lies in ignoring the digital world of our students and families. Making that choice negatively affects our ultimate responsibilities as education leaders: the teaching, learning, communicating, and connecting in our schools.

COMMUNICATE WITH PARENTS AND PATRONS

The ability to get virtually any information, anywhere, at any time is changing communities, and it is changing schools. Gone is the time when parents and patrons were willing to wait for a day, or even a week, to read a recap of graduation, the results of the volleyball tournament, or the announcement of who was hired as a new principal or coach. They expect the information to come to them quickly, and for that information to find them wherever they are.

Amy DeLaRosa is principal at Eudora Elementary School, where she administers a Facebook page for the families and supporters of the eight-hundred-plus students in her school. Having previously worked in a much smaller school and town, DeLaRosa is passionate about what social media has provided for her as a leader in both schools and communities. This is especially true as traditional newsrooms downsize—or close altogether—creating a noticeable gap in one of the most common places where people used to find information about schools. She said,

> For as long as we can remember, those of us in the schools have relied a lot on local newspapers and news stations to help us get our messages and information out in the community. As small-town newspapers are closing up shop and even newsrooms in larger cities are cutting back on staff, we are becoming less able to count on reporters for our communications to the same extent that maybe we used to.
>
> That's a big part of what makes social media so powerful. It allows us to communicate directly with our families. And in a lot of ways, it is more direct, more timely, and more reflective of our own goals and messages than traditional media ever could be.

HARNESS THE SOCIAL SHARE

Your ability to essentially short-circuit the more traditional media relationships is a powerful advantage of social media. When important information needs to be shared with families and other stakeholders as quickly as possible—an unexpected school closure, emergency, or crisis event—social media allows education leaders to craft the most accurate and transparent message. And by turning this message over to specific social media communities, you know that your message will be seen by the immediate audience, but often also—and most powerfully—shared with an audience that extends well beyond your average social media circles.

Indeed, the *social share* is what sets these digital tools apart from traditional communications tools. It is easier now than ever before for the people in your school community to take your message and share it with dozens, if not hundreds, of people they know with a simple click.

On the Eudora School District Facebook page, the average *reach* on any given post is anywhere from 750 to 1,500 people. (This useful information is provided to page administrators, along with volumes of other metrics to help better understand the page's fan base and success. We'll discuss these metrics more in chapter 7.) The most successful messages shared on the district page—often celebratory, but occasionally urgent or serious—will double, triple, or even quadruple that reach. It's all but impossible to achieve that kind of viral communication power with a newsletter, email message, or backpack flier.

Social shares—whether clicking the share button, retweeting, or sharing in other ways—constitute the very fiber of social media. People use social media sites because they want to connect to a larger group; they want to share, and to see what others are sharing. The content shared on social media ranges from news stories and interesting research to silly photos and videos—and virtually everything in between. And when we, as education leaders, create social content that is highly shareable, we gain the ability to harness a communications tool unlike anything that's ever been available to us before.

ENGAGE WITH PARENTS

Engaging families in our schools can be challenging, especially given the hectic schedules typical during the school year. When parents are required to set aside time from work or squeeze one more thing into a busy evening, attaining truly meaningful engagement can be difficult, if not impossible. But social media is a natural way to create engagement throughout the day and week, by meeting parents where they already are.

DeLaRosa said she finds that her school's parents and families are eager to engage with her social media posts, whether it's a photo of the spelling bee, a video of a kindergarten Zumba activity in P.E., or an update on the social-emotional skills being emphasized in the school from week to week. They click, share, comment, and post without hesitation, something she finds to be a powerful strategy for building relationships, connections, and ultimately, support for her school.

> Whether it was with one hundred students in my previous school, or the more than eight hundred now, social media has been the fastest and most effective way for me to connect with parents and families in the moment. I am well aware that we have families who don't use Facebook or don't have regular access to the internet, and our traditional communications pieces still allow us to reach those families like we always have. But I don't think there's a substitute for the positive, connected energy and support that I have seen generated on a social media page for a school or district. People are proud of our school, and this gives them a tangible, simple way to show that pride.

She recalled an event when the local high school basketball team qualified to play in the state tournament. It was arranged for the team bus to pull through the parking lot at her school so that the nearly one thousand students and teachers could line the sidewalks and cheer for the players as they left town. Smartphone in hand, DeLaRosa shot an eighteen-second video of the bus driving by the cheering elementary student crowd and posted it directly to the school Facebook page from her phone.

"I almost didn't even post it because the video seemed so short and simple," she said. By the end of the day, the video had a reach of nearly three thousand people—more than four thousand by the end of the next day. Not bad, especially considering the size of little Eudora, Kansas.

SUPPORT YOUR EMPLOYEES

The social media journey in Eudora Schools came about for a handful of reasons, but one of the earliest prompts arrived in the form of a request from the president of the teachers' association. As a personal Facebook user, he was connected to several other teachers in the district. Hearing the occasional, but steady, media reports about teachers losing their jobs over different social media behaviors, he also worried that some of his colleagues possibly lacked clear boundaries of how to use Facebook in a way that reflected the professional standards of education.

Certainly, the fact that this man taught in a high school further widened the gray area for him, as he reported that he and his colleagues often received friend requests from current and former students and parents. He approached the superintendent of schools to find out if there was any policy or guidelines that he could share with his members; alas, there were none.

Recognizing that this gap needed to be addressed, district leaders spent the next year working to develop the board policy and employee handbook language that now is used for every person who works in the district. This language provides a commonsense outline for our employees, which is especially helpful to the new teachers we hire right out of college each year. It creates a professional workplace that is based on clear expectations, and it provides principals and directors across the district with a specific framework for addressing questionable use of social media—whether professional or personal—that might come up.

In addition to addressing employees' personal use of social media, it was also important to acknowledge those employees who were managing social media accounts as part of their job. This included coaches who had accounts set up for their teams, sponsors who had accounts for their clubs, and teachers who had accounts for parents and students. For some time, these accounts had been allowed to exist without great concern, based on the integrity of the professionals who were managing them.

However, without a formal social media approach, these employees were operating without either oversight or support. It is problematic for school and district leaders to intervene in a social media page managed by a coach or teacher, if that employee is doing the work on his or her own time, off the district network. (And if school internet filters are set up to block Facebook, employees are left little other choice than to manage pages from home.) Weaving social media into the culture of a workplace gives employees clear expectations to help ensure appropriate personal behavior online; it also gives administrators a concrete role in the oversight and guidance when there is a professional presence online.

PROTECT YOUR REPUTATION

From the smallest towns to the largest cities, the digital world has fundamentally changed communication expectations. Not only do the majority of district parents, patrons, and older students have access to the internet from anywhere at any time, but they also have an expectation that the information most important to them will come to them on their terms. *If a school system doesn't meet this expectation, someone else will take charge of the information flow to fill in the gap.*

A school system without an intentional and coordinated social media presence is seriously and even dangerously vulnerable to being falsely represented by someone else. And whether it's a well-meaning PTO mom, or a not-so-well-meaning student, employee, or community member, if you aren't the voice that is representing your school or district, you have a problem.

In many cases, the self-appointed representative does well for a time but then stops posting updates, making the school or district look outdated and unresponsive. On a much more serious level, you must actively address the potential for an ugly, mean-spirited, or negative site to come up when people enter your school's or district's name in a search engine. Nothing less than your system's reputation and public image are at stake.

People searching to find you on social media have little way of knowing whether pages called "Central School District" or "James Madison Elementary" are, or are not, truly managed by representatives of those organizations. Even if your school or district isn't yet ready to actively use social media, you should, at a minimum, take the time to search popular social networks to find out if rogue accounts exist and report them as abusive if they do. (Social media companies all have very simple reporting procedures built into their sites for this purpose.)

Once you have identified and reported rogue accounts, it's well worth the extra effort to establish your own profiles on Facebook, Twitter, Instagram, YouTube, Google+, Pinterest, LinkedIn, and others. Reserving the profile of both your schools and the district in these social media spaces will go a long way in preventing someone else from falsely assuming your identity. Take it one step further and, for each "name holder" profile you set up, find a way to post information about your school and/or district, such as:

> *Thanks for visiting James Madison Elementary. We aren't currently using [Facebook/Twitter/YouTube/etc.], but you can find us online at www.JamesMadisonElementary.org or call us at 999-555-4444.*

By reserving your name and posting this very basic information, you have created a strong safeguard against being misrepresented by others on social media. As you go through this process, be careful to document each site with the corresponding login information so that you can get back in when you're ready to begin actively using your accounts.

As a general practice, school leaders should set up email alerts with keywords, so that they are notified when the school or district is being discussed on social media. (Google News Alerts and Mention.com are two good, free or low-cost resources for this.) Leaders also must regularly audit the accounts appearing when using the search bar on social media sites and typing in the name of your school, or other local keywords. This can be done by anyone in an office setting, as long as the person has proper filter access and understands the types of impostor or rogue accounts to watch for.

These audits should be performed at least twice a year or, more preferably, on a monthly or quarterly basis. Additionally, any information about a possible rogue or abusive account that comes to you from an employee, student, or parent should be taken seriously and investigated without delay. Your school's and/or district's ability to protect your image and communicate important messages with credibility and clarity absolutely hinges on your vigilance.

When social media is used as a communications tool, it works very much like a traditional town hall meeting or an informal stop by the local coffee shop to chat with parents and patrons. What sets social media apart from these other traditional communications approaches, though, is that it reaches a much larger group of people, right where they are.

If you knew that fifty, five hundred, or five thousand of your parents and patrons were going to be sitting around socializing at the local community center at ten o'clock on a Tuesday morning, wouldn't you take the opportunity to drop by and talk about your schools? If you heard that tonight your schools' influencers and opinion leaders would be gathering in the diner with the blue awning, rather than the diner with the red awning, you'd know where to go to get your message out. If you knew that your stakeholders showed up at a playground every Saturday morning at 9:30, you'd make it a point to drop by when there was news to share.

This is social media. This is where your parents and community members are, multiple times throughout the day, in numbers that might even astound you. Go there.

KEY IDEAS TO REMEMBER

- The way that students and families learn, connect, and engage has changed. It is up to education leaders to find ways to formally welcome the digital world inside schools and classrooms in order to continue to meet the needs of students and families.
- The risks of embracing social media can be managed through intentionally crafted policies, procedures, and professional development programs.
- Because of the way that people communicate and share information on social media, these tools offer school systems enormous potential to engage patrons, parents, and students in ways that build relationships and increase support.
- Regardless of the approach to system-wide social media, education leaders must take steps now to protect the online reputation of their schools and districts by reserving accounts and establishing methods of monitoring social media activity based on relevant keywords.

NOTES

1. "The U.S. Digital Consumer Report," February 10, 2014, http://www.nielsen.com/us/en/reports/2014/the-us-digital-consumer-report.html.
2. January 17, 2017, http://www.nielsen.com/us/en/insights/reports/2017/2016-nielsen-social-media-report.html.

TWO

Why Are We Afraid?

When the topic of social media comes up in certain education circles, the discussion is focused on excitement, innovation, and opportunity. But more often, the prospect of bringing the digital world inside our classroom stirs concerns and genuine fears. Each of these points of view is exactly right, and thoughtful risk management is the key to finding a way to bring them together.

Risk management is the language of leaders—superintendents, board members, and principals. Formal policies, procedures, and professional development efforts can mitigate the risks of social media, while clearly resonating with key decision makers in a school system. But first, it's critical that education leaders interested in embracing the social media shift understand the reasons why many people are still quite uncomfortable with the idea of welcoming social media in schools.

ANGRY PEOPLE WILL MAKE US LOOK BAD

For education leaders, two-way communication is essential to creating the transparency and trust that, in turn, generate support for schools. It involves sharing information, and it demands listening to what families, employees, and other stakeholder groups think.

Beyond sharing, two-way communication requires leaders to listen, explain, think, acknowledge, encourage, apologize, congratulate, and respond. Sometimes it's fun and easy, such as the chance to celebrate a National Merit Finalist or state championship. Other times, it's more nuanced, such as questions about a change in policy. And sometimes it is downright challenging, such as acknowledging a failure in handling a crisis, or people angry about the use of their tax dollars.

11

Anyone who has facilitated a town hall meeting or parent focus group knows that two-way communication isn't always easy and comfortable. And while two-way sharing is the very reason people are so attracted to social media, it's also what makes it so scary to many education leaders. Here are some fears and concerns commonly expressed by leaders about the use of such a public, online tool for two-way communication:

- What if someone makes a negative comment?
- What if someone posts something that violates the confidentiality of one of our students?
- What if someone posts something bad about a staff member?
- What if one of our employees posts something unprofessional?
- What if it becomes a place where people go to air dirty laundry, or crank up the rumor mill?

These all are legitimate fears and important considerations when a school district gets involved in social media, and much of this book is dedicated to specific ways to help address these concerns. But the important thing to understand right now is that *these things are already happening on social media.*

Indeed, somebody, somewhere, is already posting their latest gripe over student fees, a disciplinary decision, or a principal who knowingly allows bullying. Somebody is already naming the person who hurt a child and criticizing the school leaders for not doing more. Somebody is already posting inaccurate information about your upcoming ballot issue or the superintendent's fringe benefits. By making the choice *not* to use social media, you are not exempting yourself from the discussions taking place on social media; by contrast, you are allowing those discussions to flourish unchecked and without your consistent, informed, and calming voice.

Again, these concerns are well grounded, and education leaders must take the time to develop thoughtful and clear protocol to handle negative, nasty, or otherwise inappropriate comments. But the good news is that staking out space for your school or district on social media creates an environment where these types of comments and issues rarely come up—and where they are dealt with in a manner that is respectful, understanding, firm, and policy-driven.

Certainly there are instances where private social media groups fuel negative—at times arguably toxic—conversations about your school. As a leader, it's critical that you pay attention to these groups and understand both the issues and the participants involved. However, it is not advised that you actively participate in these groups, or use them to post a response of any kind.

It is unwise to create any perception that a private social media group is a place where leaders will solve problems; you have existing district channels and procedures for that. However, awareness of these conversations allows you to take a range of appropriate steps that can help you to better understand the dynamic, and ideally influence a less hostile dynamic moving forward. While it would be unethical to plant someone in a private group or create a fake account to become a member, there are appropriate relationship-based strategies that can help change the conversation over time:

- Find out who the group moderators are, and initiate a personal conversation by phone or face to face. Often a group with an inflammatory conversation is led by positive or neutral community members. A conversation may uncover ways that you can work together to improve official communication processes and possibly improve the tone within the group.
- Determine if there are "good guys" in the group—the people who routinely serve on your committees or volunteer in the school. If privately approached, these individuals may be willing to speak up on behalf of the district—even withstand pushback from others—if they feel confident that they have the facts straight. It's remarkable to see how one positive or factual comment can bring out others in support of the school system and its leaders.
- If possible, screen capture any comment thread that mentions an employee or student by name. If you are not a member of the group but were contacted about these types of comments, ask the person who contacted you to send you screenshots for appropriate documentation.
- Remember that some of the conversations that burn hottest, also burn themselves out after a few hours or a few days. If an angry discussion about the school is the exception to the group's normal activity, it may be best to allow it to resolve itself, and monitor it in case it does not.

When two-way communication gets uncomfortable, school leaders should take a page from the corporate playbook. For nearly a decade, companies and major brands have been pioneering two-way communication on social media. And the ones that use it successfully don't avoid confrontation—instead, they use those moments as opportunities to increase brand loyalty.

Imagine coming home from the store with a cup of Chobani Greek yogurt. The very next day, you open it for breakfast only to discover that it is spoiled, but instead of calling a phone number or sending a letter, you log on to Twitter and tweet them your concern. Or perhaps the plane ticket you bought from Southwest Airlines as a Christmas surprise for your mother-in-law isn't allowing her to check in and reserve her boarding position. Again, instead of making a phone call, composing a letter, or even sending an email, you go on Southwest's Facebook page and post your panicked (and probably peeved) question.

The best companies on social media have truly mastered the ability to find solutions when customers are disappointed, confused, angry—even irrational—while building loyalty, trust, and respect for their brand. If businesses can handle angry customers from around the world, education leaders can absolutely handle the challenging posts from the people in our school district.

WE NEED FILTERS TO PROTECT US

There are a host of reasons why internet filters have an important place on school district networks. Most critically, they help protect students from inappropriate, even dangerous, content that is available across the World Wide Web—and many websites containing that content are blocked for very good reason.

Nobody could argue that sites with pornography or violence add any value to, or have any place in, a school's teaching and learning environment. But there are so many sites—Facebook, Twitter, YouTube, Instagram, blog platforms, and others—that offer enormous opportunities for teachers and students, but often are blocked by district filters. Frequently, people who are uncomfortable with social media in schools will suggest that students can reap equally important benefits by using work-around sites tailored to classroom use—sites that mimic the most popular social media sites but are not visible to the public, or sites that closely regulate content.

While these education-focused sites may be useful in some situations, a good deal of the power of social media in the classroom is the instant relevance that is created when the same platforms that are used in the classroom are used in the world outside our schools. Furthermore, an unmatched layer of expectation and accountability is added when students know that their words and work will be visible to the public—all over the world.

Some who support using district internet filters to block social media sites fear that employees will be too distracted if they can log in to those sites at school. "If we let our people on Facebook," they argue, "they'll spend too much time at work chatting with friends." This concern, however, is not a social media problem, but rather a simple human resources issue. Employees have myriad ways to be distracted at work on any given day. They have district-issued phones at their desk or in a nearby workspace. They have personal cell phones in their purse or pocket. They share workrooms and lunchrooms with colleagues. If someone wants to chat all day with friends, blocking social media certainly won't eliminate that distraction.

Let's face it: In the smartphone world where we now live, employees (and, quite frankly, most teen and many tweens) already can access virtually any social network from the palm of their hand, using the most basic cellular data plan. Internet filtering has a solid place in schools and will continue to play an indispensable role in keeping highly inappropriate content out of classrooms. But it is time for education leaders to acknowledge that using filters to shut out social media is both ineffective and shortsighted.

UGLY HEADLINES

As long as there have been teachers in schools, a few have made questionable choices in their interactions with other students, colleagues, or parents. Most often the choices are less a reflection of an employee's character and more an illustration of the fact that teachers and all employees are, of course, human. Examples might include dropping a four-letter word during a heated discussion with a parent, being overheard at the local bar and grill complaining about a bad day, or displaying a photo from a summer family reunion that shows someone drinking beer.

In rare cases, however, the questionable choices are much more serious, even criminal. Not only do social networks provide a space where inappropriate activity can take place, but these cases also amplify the attention that such behavior gets when it is discovered. There isn't an education leader out there—or anyone working in schools in any position—who doesn't cringe at least a little when a report comes on the news about a teacher getting in trouble for inappropriate behavior on social media.

Greg Gorman, superintendent of a very small school district in rural Kansas, is one leader who has found value in embracing social media, despite the fears. "The biggest threat I think you will find is a generational issue," he said. "It comes from people in my age bracket—which is old—mostly because they aren't a part of social media, they don't understand it, or they only believe in the negative publicity that the media portrays about it."

Stories of teachers losing their jobs and hurting innocent people with their actions are enough to make any educator nervous. As mentioned in chapter 1, it was the Eudora Schools teachers' association president who first raised concerns about his colleagues' presence on social media. This sparked the work to design guidelines and professional development plans to support employees while encouraging the use of social media among administrators, staff members, and students.

We will discuss the approach to professional development in greater depth in chapter 6, but the guidelines and expectations that you will establish throughout this process will go a long way in protecting your employees. This work also will help reduce the chances that you will turn on the evening news and see a story about the reckless online behavior of one of your teachers or other employees.

And once again it must be noted: A critical mass of your employees are already on social media sites outside of work. Refusing to embrace social media in your district or school does not decrease the chance of your employees making a poor choice online. In fact, shutting out social media only increases the chance of something negative happening if they have never been taught the risks, expectations, and consequences for online behavior that you have for those working in your school system.

News coverage can pose a frustrating challenge to administrators and teacher leaders who are working to convince the top decision makers to be open to the shift to social media. Stories of the dangers of social media often create and reinforce a great deal of ongoing fear and concern among leaders who insist that social media is too risky for schools. If you find yourself working against the tide of negative news with the decision makers in your school or district, here are some strategies to consider:

- Articulate the "why" of social media in your schools. Frame your ideas and vision within the constructs of existing goals and priorities. See where social media aligns with your mission statement, strategic plan, or other important area of focus. Doing this illustrates the fact that embracing social media isn't just "one more thing" or another fad, but rather, something that weaves through and supports the leader's other top goals, such as student engagement, employee trust, and community support.
- Highlight a nearby district or school that is using social media successfully. Giving examples or hearing positive experiences from other districts will show social media in action in a reassuring, nonthreatening way. Show how positive it can be, but also take the time to find out the biggest fears and challenges that the district faces in using it. Telling the whole story—both good and bad—will make your case more compelling, and it will show that even the challenges, when handled with a little intentional effort, are manageable.
- Make a plan. If you believe the leader is more reluctant about the shift than outright opposed to it, ask if you could develop a short summary of why the social media shift is important, touching on everything from student learning to protection of the school or district's online reputation. It should also include a recommendation to form a collaborative work group with a diverse array of job titles and functions that will examine the opportunities and risks in your school or district, and then recommend next steps to manage those risks and embrace the opportunities. We will discuss this collaboration process more in the next chapter.

- Be patient. Keep in mind that it takes time to influence someone's attitudes and opinions, especially if those attitudes are regularly reinforced by close advisors, friends, or family members—or by frequent negative reports in the media. If a top leader is clearly unwilling to consider the shift, look for someone close to the leader who might be more open to it. Working with someone the leader already trusts is one way to help people warm up to new or uncomfortable ideas over time. This might also be someone who would be open to receiving your proposal or thinking through the collaborative process that will follow.

The digital world is constantly changing, and the shifts that must be made in response to these changes can feel overwhelming on good days—and downright scary on others. Fears are a natural part of change, but education leaders are at their best when they see the real opportunities to make a difference for students, families, and colleagues. When the opportunity for good is as big as it is in the social media embrace, the fears we have should no longer control our decisions. Instead, it's time to open our minds to the shift, and open the doors for great things to happen.

Andrea Gribble is a speaker and CEO of #SocialSchool4EDU, a company that provides encouragement, support, and social media management services to dozens of districts across the United States. She founded her company with the express purpose of helping school districts spread good news in their community. "In a time that has so much negativity, the world needs the stories from our schools," she said. "Social media can truly change the world in a positive way, and when we use it in our schools, we can teach our students to use it for good. This is a chance to change the world, and we need to make the most of it."

KEY IDEAS TO REMEMBER

- There are many legitimate reasons why education leaders may be uncomfortable with embracing social media in a school system, and understanding these fears or concerns is critical to finding a path forward.
- The fear of negative, untrue, or damaging comments being made on social media about the school, district, or an employee is well founded. However, these kinds of comments are already happening on social media sites that aren't under your control. By carving an official and active space in social media, you can help clarify and redirect many such commenters and conversations.
- It is normal for private social media groups to form and sometimes include angry criticism of schools. Resist the temptation to engage with these groups. Instead, use simple relationship strategies to

help address concerns through appropriate processes, and help guide the tone of the group's discussion to one of understanding and meaningful problem-solving.

- Network filters are useful to keep students safe on district devices at school. But in the world of mobile devices, education leaders must acknowledge that blocking social media sites is no longer as useful as educating students about how to use them appropriately.
- Nobody enjoys stories about school employees making poor choices on social media sites. The best way to decrease the chances of having your employee in such a story is to provide specific guidelines and intentional professional development about appropriate use and important security settings.
- If colleagues or district leaders are strongly influenced by the news coverage of social media problems, there are steps to help normalize their view of these digital tools and move the conversation forward.

THREE

Getting Started

A high school teacher once half-jokingly referred to "moving at the speed of education" when it comes to the sometimes painfully slow rate of change in a school system. And indeed, big changes (and even some small ones) in a K–12 system rarely happen overnight, or even over the course of a school year. The process of changing a system as complex and dynamic as a school system—whether it's curriculum, procedures, or policies—requires both hard work and patience, because the changes involve such critical elements as attitudes, behaviors, and expectations.

The social media shift is no different, especially when you consider the legitimate fears and obstacles outlined in the previous chapter. Indeed, when people in a system are concerned or anxious about change, the process can slow down almost to a standstill. Whether it's moving quickly, slowly, or barely at all, your role as an education leader is to prevent it from stopping altogether. When you are in the thick of a systems change, take a cue from Dory, the irrepressibly optimistic travel companion in the Walt Disney/Pixar classic *Finding Nemo*: "Just keep swimming, just keep swimming, just keep swimming, swimming, swimming."

While it's easy to feel discouraged by the slow rate of change, keep in mind that there are two distinct advantages to the process and shift prompted by bringing social media into our schools. First—and most importantly—this change plays to the natural culture of schools, filled with a wide range of invested, caring individuals who typically are quite passionate about opportunities for students to learn, grow, and experience the world in new ways.

But also, where social media is concerned, many of these employees also have a personal knowledge of Facebook, or any number of social media sites. As a result, there are probably people in your system who are primed to embrace social media, and perhaps help you lead a social media shift in your district or school. These may be the ones, described in the first chapter, who are managing work-related social media accounts on their own time. Or they may simply be people who are excited about the opportunities they have heard about and are waiting for permission to get started.

Inevitably, there also will be some people in your school or district who are dreading a change. They may feel overwhelmed by such a shift, have a negative bias toward social media, or simply be nervous, as many leaders are about the risks and the unknown. (Although the Eudora School District now has a well-established history embracing social media for communication, teaching, and learning, there remain teachers who are active users of social media in their personal lives, but who are reluctant, for one reason or another, to use it for work. Changing large systems takes patience.) Regardless of where your employees are on this spectrum, it's important to remember to frame your work process around the thing that most genuinely motivates school employees: doing what is best for kids.

ARTICULATE YOUR VISION

As you lead the change in your school or district, the first step is to establish your vision by answering these three questions:

Where Do You Want to Go?

What will the first stage of your school or district's social media embrace look like when it is complete? Keep in mind that systems change best in phases, so it's wise to break down a big vision—"Every teacher and coach will use a social media account to enrich student learning and communicate with students and/or parents"—into more achievable chunks of work. The first-stage goal in Eudora was to ensure that everyone working in the schools was encouraged to take advantage of the professional opportunities afforded them by social media. Equally important at this point was ensuring that all employees clearly understood the district's expectations for appropriate use of social media (at work and on personal time), and how to mitigate the unique set of risks that social media presents, both personally and professionally.

What Are Your Opportunities?

Think broadly, including such areas as student learning, professional growth for teachers, and communication with families and other stakeholder groups. Eudora leaders were particularly focused on opening up opportunities for teachers to use social media as an instructional tool, as well as opening up additional lines of communication with parents and patrons. Professional development and networking opportunities for teachers were quickly added to the list of opportunities, as well.

What Are Your Challenges or Barriers?

There are, of course, the typical challenges of fear and resistance to change. As you plan, work to articulate these fears as specifically as you can. Are people most afraid of negative comments, professional liability, getting in over their heads? Or is it a more generalized fear of what they've heard on the news, or perhaps simply a generalized resistance to change?

Then, think about how your district operates—apart from the natural fears and resistance, identify the other challenges that must be confronted as you prepare to embrace the social media shift. If the embrace were to kick off tomorrow, what wouldn't work? In Eudora, we needed to address network filters, as well as the capacity for wireless access and internet traffic. Underperformance of bandwidth, in fact, had been an ongoing problem that was being addressed; district leaders certainly didn't want to make an existing problem worse with new changes.

While you can approach these questions working on your own, it's ideal and helpful to invite one or two others who are already open to social media in schools. Included in this group should be at least one top-level leader, or perhaps a person who is trusted by—and influential with—the top-level leaders in your district, and whose blessing can help move your work forward. Working in a small group will allow you to more fully answer each question and thoroughly probe the issues to find weak spots.

The more work you do with this small group, and the more time you spend on these three questions, the better prepared you will be when it's time to move into the more active work mode.

GROW YOUR GROUP

Once your small group has established a clear vision for your school or district's social media shift, it's time to expand your collaboration. This group will grow and change; do not confuse it with a committee or task force, but rather an ever-widening group of stakeholders where you are building consensus and refining your vision. In Eudora, this initial groundwork began with the superintendent and communications director; the district's technology director, building principals, and curriculum director were brought on board as the work progressed.

Throughout this process, feedback and advice were sought from Ben Smith, a nearby business owner whose company, Social:IRL, advises companies large and small in social media strategy. Smith's influence and expertise were invaluable, particularly in Eudora leaders' focus on framing the social media embrace around seizing opportunity and mitigating risks.

Undoubtedly, Smith's contract work with Eudora Schools for the first few years was an enormous asset, but it's unrealistic to assume that every school system would have access to such a consultant. Fortunately, a great deal of what was learned through this relationship is reflected in the policies, procedures, and professional development approaches shared in this book; the exploration of these key areas in subsequent chapters will bring you much of the benefit that Smith brought to Eudora leaders.

Make no mistake: Having the superintendent of schools involved from the very first meaningful discussion was critical in Eudora, transforming the initial efforts to move forward with concrete directives from the top district leader. If, instead of a top leader, your vision process includes someone close to him or her, this is the time to begin having conversations about how to engage your superintendent in the process. Prepare a plan to secure his or her buy-in before moving forward and expanding the scope of your group's participants.

At this stage in your work, and once you have established the support of the leader or leaders whose permission you will need, it's also important to note that the vision and goal-setting work is complete for now. As new people are included in conversations, the expectation should remain clear: We are embracing social media. The questions to work through are why, how, who, and when—*not* if. Instead of asking, *What do you think?* leaders and facilitators should focus on the question, *What do you need?*

At every step throughout this process, you are proposing a new idea—a system change—each time you bring it to a new person, or a new group of people. Up to this point, you have probably mostly included the "easy sell" colleagues in your work, which is absolutely the right way to build early momentum. But as you begin including people by function—technology department, legal department, principals, teachers' association, and so on—you will likely have a mix of attitudes about embracing social media.

For this reason, it's important to lead each new conversation by describing the changes that have taken place in the digital world, including both online social sharing communities and the wave of mobile access through smartphones and tablets. A short internet search will reveal the latest statistics on how children and families are using social media and mobile technology; use this information to illustrate how your students are living one world outside of school and another world inside of school.

In Eudora, a two-minute animated slideshow was created to make this point and was played each time the discussion circle grew. The slideshow, which flies through a battery of eye-opening statistics about digital trends that relate to our students and families, was a powerful way to draw attention to the gaps between the world where our students and families live and the education world, and how people in the district must adapt in order to remain relevant, challenging, and effective.

Once you present the case for why it's time for change, it's time to present the big-picture idea in the most striking way possible—letting your group members know that there are great opportunities that have not yet been seized:

- Describe the variety of social media sites that are available and ready to use as yet-untapped *free* resources for teaching and learning.
- Share feedback you have from parents about the school information they wish they had more of.
- Refer to the employees who have already expressed interest in using social media. Mention the ones who are already using it for their jobs, but without any professional development, support, or accountability from their supervisor.

The work of this larger group is to understand the vision you already have articulated and to help you refine that vision by sharing their range of reactions and perspectives. As you reflect on the opportunities above, your group members can continue open-ended discussions about their interests in embracing social media, as well as their fears.

To effectively lead your colleagues through this change process, embrace the times when you can listen to and acknowledge a person's fears. Although it may not be a fear of yours—or even seem a bit far-fetched from your point of view—being present in those moments and facilitating a constructive, safe discussion is a powerful way to keep everyone moving forward. Rest assured in the knowledge that all the risks of social media can be managed; your job right now is to let people express their concerns and reassure them that policies, procedures, and professional development programs will be developed to address those very fears.

TEST THE WATERS

At an early point in your ever-growing group's work, spend the time to do two short surveys: one with employees and another with students' parents. Survey data can be incredibly helpful as you discern your next steps and develop your plan. It can also be quite compelling to those who are reluctant to move ahead in embracing social media in the school when they see that key groups of individuals are ready, interested, and asking for it.

Data resonates strongly with top-level leaders, so surveys can be a great tool for building that critical support. Furthermore, understanding your employees' perceptions, ideas, and fears also will be valuable as you begin to plan the professional development for your initiative.

Administering a survey can be as simple as writing a few questions on a free or low-cost online survey tool—Google Forms and SurveyMonkey are two popular choices—and sending a link by email to the target group. And, if the survey is relatively short and straightforward, you need not allow more than one week for respondents to complete it.

One word of caution: As an education leader, do not send out a survey on social media unless and until you are confident that your initiative is genuinely moving forward, with the support of key leaders. If people view you as someone who is "in the know," or someone who has influence on the school's or district's policy decisions, sending out a survey will be perceived as steps toward adoption and change. Avoid implying that this is the path the school or district is taking in the very near future, until it truly is.

Here are a few key questions for employees:

- Do you currently use social media for your own personal enjoyment or entertainment?
- Do you feel confident about how your personal use of social media may influence your role as a school employee?
- Do you currently use social media as part of your school district job or role as a professional?
- Do you believe that professional use of social media could be helpful to you in your job?
- If our (school/district) were to begin embracing the use of social media at work, what do you believe might be the most exciting opportunity? What would be your biggest concern?
- What kind of training would you hope to receive before using social media in your job?

Here are a few key questions for parents and families:

- What kind of information do you most enjoy or appreciate receiving from our (school/district)?
- What kind of (school/district) information do you wish you received more of?
- Do you, or does your spouse, currently use social media to get information on a daily or nearly daily basis?
- What social network do you and/or your spouse most regularly use?

- If our (school/district) were to use social media as one tool for communicating with parents and families, would you find that helpful?
- Do you have any concerns or fears about our (school/district) using social media to communicate with parents and families?

As your collaborative group grows, there will come a point when it's time to move forward on a system level; in Eudora, this point came when all district principals and directors had been involved in the discussions, and that feedback had been used to refine the district's vision and outline an action plan. This group helped review and improve proposed guidelines for district employees and board policy language, as well as identify needs and ideas for professional development. Again, this process was greatly informed by the collaboration with Ben Smith, and the results of that work are reflected and made available throughout this book.

As the feedback group grows to the point that most key leaders and influencers are involved, it is time to shift into work mode and begin developing the policy, procedures, and professional development. These three things will function as the foundation of your risk management approach to a social media embrace; each of them will be explored in depth over the next three chapters.

KEY IDEAS TO REMEMBER

- The first step to lead the social shift in a school system is to define the vision and identify both the opportunities and barriers involved with moving ahead.
- It is best for the change process to begin in a small group of no more than three or four people. Once this group has articulated the vision and explored the opportunities and barriers, additional stake-
holders should be added and included in the discussions.
- As the group grows, all discussions should raise the question, *What do you need?* while carefully avoiding the question, *What do you think?* With a vision already in place, the work should not focus on whether the shift should happen, but rather, how to support and guide people as it happens.
- Survey data, even when collected with free online tools, can be a compelling tool to demonstrate the existing use of social media by parents, students, and employees. The feedback also can help identify areas of opportunity, as well as areas of concern that should be addressed in the design of policies, procedures, and professional development.

FOUR

Policy

Expectations and Consequences

How many times have you been aware of a situation that involves social media and an employee, student, or parent—one that you know is causing problems—but you were uncertain anything could be done? Or worse yet, you *knew* nothing could be done? Having sound, well-written policies in place can untie your hands to make a positive difference, and they are an essential piece of the work to bring social media into your schools and classrooms.

Without question, school board policy is the backbone for everything that happens in school districts each day. Policy gives employees both direction and boundaries, and it gives school board members and other top leaders a framework to both define expectations and manage risk. Just as when you create a new administrative structure or update your crisis response plan, this framework must be in place as you work toward a full embrace of social media in your schools and district. Without it, your initiative will be missing the support of the board and is unlikely to take hold across different groups of people or over any length of time.

WRITING YOUR POLICY

The fundamental goal of policy is to outline both expectations and consequences, and social media policy should do exactly that. Begin by reviewing the policy that already exists in your district. There likely already exists at least one policy, or a policy structure, where social media objectives will fit. Keep in mind in this work that your approach to social media must encompass employee use of social media, but it also should cover student and even parent uses as they relate to the school environment. As you examine existing policy, look for opportunities where additions or adaptations can address these specific areas:

- Appropriate use of social media by employees at the workplace, during the workday, and/or on district equipment;
- Appropriate use of social media by employees outside of the workplace or workday, and/or on personal equipment;
- Expectations and consequences for students and/or parents using social media as a means to bully or otherwise disrupt the school learning environment.

The Eudora Board of Education first adopted a policy in 2014, but soon found that it was nearly impossible to enforce the daily use of social media by employees. The notion that social media sites should be used *only* for work purposes ignores the reality of social media in general.

Consider a teacher who is tweeting with his or her high school Spanish class as part of a student learning activity. If that teacher happens to see a tweet that is unrelated to classwork—a favorite sports team or pet adoption photo, for example—it is a natural inclination to take a moment to click that tweet. The notion that a principal or other supervisor would be able to enforce that type of policy was not reasonable.

To their credit, board members agreed that a social media policy should allow for the occasional personal use of social media during the day by an employee. After all, teachers and staff occasionally place or accept a personal call during the workday—an update from the car mechanic or a question for the family pediatrician. This revised policy was adopted in 2014 to better outline reasonable—and enforceable—expectations for employee use of social media.

> This policy applies to all social media activities by district employees, including but not limited to the use of blogs, forums, social networking sites (e.g., Facebook, Twitter, LinkedIn, Google+, Flickr, Tumblr, and YouTube), and any other web-based communications on publicly available sites. These activities are encouraged to take place in a classroom or school office setting so long as such activities do not detract from the employees' effectiveness or other job duties.
>
> When participating in social media activities, even off duty and off premises, such activities must not violate any Board policies or otherwise interfere with the employee's or coworkers' job performance. The Board expects all employees to exercise professionalism and good judgment in any social media activities, as outlined in the Social Media Guidelines for District Employees. Furthermore, any social media activities must comply with all applicable laws including, but not limited to, anti-discrimination, anti-harassment, copyright, trademark, defamation, privacy, securities, and any other applicable laws and regulations.

Any violation of this policy, of the Social Media Guidelines for District Employees, or of any Board policies or procedures as a result of social media activities, may result in corrective action, up to and including termination.

The superintendent is responsible for recommending social media guidelines for approval by the Board.

Keep in mind that social media sites, as well as laws and regulations, are constantly changing. As with all policy, leaders should work with legal counsel to determine the language most appropriate to an individual district's structure, value, and goals.

BULLYING AND SOCIAL MEDIA

While it's not always thought of as traditional bullying, cyberbullying is a very real problem—and the consequences of it can pose an even greater danger to the well-being of your students and employees. Typically, one required element in the definition of bullying is the repeated incidence of intentional teasing or meanness that a person experiences over a period of time. What makes cyberbullying so damaging is the fact that single tweets, Instagram photos, and Facebook posts are much different than a single comment on the bus or in the school hallway.

As discussed already, the very power of social media exists in its sharing nature, where one piece of content can be seen and shared dozens, hundreds, or even thousands of times over. Even a "private" post can be screen captured, copied and pasted, or otherwise shared with others. Consequently, the permanence of a single post on social media far exceeds the permanence of a single comment at school.

Education leaders must acknowledge that cyberbullying *does happen*, that it is most likely already happening in their schools, and that it is a legitimate risk to address in the embrace of social media. (Indeed, even districts still unwilling to embrace social media in the classroom should adapt to at least protect students and employees from the damage of cyberbullying.)

Every state in the United States has laws and/or policies directing school boards to protect students from bullying, and many states also require these to include cyberbullying. However, it is incredibly important in the digital age that education leaders do what they can to also protect the employees in their schools from bullying on social media. While adults working in a school might be considered unlikely targets for bullying in the traditional sense, the scope of social media turns this assumption on its head.

With the sharing power and instant connectivity of social media, statements or other content that a student or parent posts about a district employee have permanence in a way that they never did before, greatly

increasing their potential damage. It takes no more than one post accusing a teacher of sexual misconduct with a student to potentially destroy
that professional's working environment, short-circuiting any opportunity for an administrator to conduct an investigation and handle the concerns respectfully and confidentially.

School district employees are entitled to protection from threats of
cyberbullying, just as students are, and policy and guidelines are the
place to formalize this priority. If your district's policies do not already
include these kinds of protections, now is the time to make that recommendation.

HANDBOOK GUIDELINES FOR EMPLOYEES

Understanding that the individuals who make up your team of employees will bring with them a wide range of experience and understanding
of social media, handbook guidelines are an essential tool that allows you
to educate your teachers and other staff members.

In preparing guidelines, consider this: Educators spend a great deal of
time and effort teaching students what is expected of them and then
rewarding or correcting them if those expectations are not met. Similarly,
it only makes sense that employees would also be taught what is expected from them on social media, and what the consequences will be if
those expectations are not met.

Indeed, social media guidelines for employees are a teaching tool, first
and foremost. Just as with policy, board-adopted handbook guidelines
are an important piece of a well-informed, positive, and systematic approach to social media. There is no shortage of examples of prohibitive
and restrictive policies for employee use of social media, but your goal in
facilitating a social media shift in your schools is the opposite—instead of
reinforcing a climate of fear and avoidance, you are working to create a
professional environment of wisdom, trust, and openness to opportunity.

Remember, your goal is not to scare employees away from using social media in their practice, but rather to give them a framework where
they feel comfortable and confident using it to connect with students,
parents, and patrons in new and meaningful ways. Employee guidelines,
when approved by the board and reflected in board policy, are where this
distinction will make an enormous difference.

As Voltaire wrote, "Common sense is not so common." There likely
will be elements of your guidelines that, to some, will seem like common
sense. As you develop your policies, however, remember that the average social media user often lacks some basic understanding when it
comes to how social media sites really work. And these misunderstandings often can lead to problems if they are not intentionally addressed.

Teachers who are new to the profession benefit from having specific expectations spelled out for them as they transition from the college lifestyle to a lifestyle as a school district professional. But even experienced teachers, who first encountered social media well into adulthood, often have a fair amount to learn about how a person's social media presence is always permanent and never truly private. Well-written guidelines offer every employee the support they need and deserve.

Social media strategist and advisor to Eudora leaders, Ben Smith, offers an important perspective: "You must switch the mindset to stop living in fear of doing something wrong, and start empowering people to do something good. People want boundaries, they want guidance, they want to know how to use social media well."

Here are just a few of the employee questions—and corresponding answers—that can be overheard in virtually any school system, large or small:

- Everyone I know posts about a bad day at work—why is this different for me? (Fact: It matters a great deal when you work in a school, from issues of privacy and confidentiality to a person's professional reputation and/or the school or district's reputation and liability.)
- I get Facebook friend requests from my students all the time, but I never know if I should accept them or not. Some other students want me to follow them on Instagram. It makes me really uncomfortable. (Fact: While employees are allowed to connect on social networks with whomever they choose, they should be encouraged to think twice, understanding that there will be an added level of responsibility and scrutiny applied to them. If they choose to connect with students, they should be encouraged to be consistent with all similar requests, to avoid any appearance of favoritism. They must also refrain from using private message features to communicate with students or parents; only sanctioned messaging tools, such as district email, should be used for student communication.)
- If I post a less-than-professional photo of myself from an after-hours party during spring break, why does it matter? I posted it on my personal Facebook page—it's not like I was (smoking a cigarette/drinking a beer/wearing revealing clothing) at school. (Fact: Who you are online is the same as who you are in real life. If you wouldn't want your student's parent, your boss, or a school board member to see it, do not post it. Period.)
- If I post something and then take it down, it goes away forever, right? (Fact: Nothing posted ever really goes away. Even if it's only up for a moment, it could be screen captured, photographed, shared, or saved. All tweets are archived by the Library of Congress, and the FTC allows private corporations to store publicly

accessible social media posts for as many as seven years to be used in employee background checks for future or current employers.)

- I use privacy settings to make sure only my very closest friends and family can find me on social media, so why does it matter what I post there? (Fact: Your very closest friends and family may not always understand or share your commitment to privacy and could easily screen capture, copy and paste, or refer to your post in a much more public way.)

As an education leader, you must be mindful about maintaining your supportive, forward-thinking approach as you work to address all the questions that your employees will inevitably have regarding their use of social media. With policies that clearly define and explain your expectations, guidelines become the tool for employees to use in making good decisions, often avoiding altogether these types of naive and potentially risky assumptions.

Effective employee guidelines will better equip your employees to make smart decisions in their online activity, both personally and professionally. But again, social media is about so much more than risk. Your ultimate goal in embracing the social media shift in your schools is not merely about risk avoidance—it's much more importantly about empowerment and opportunity.

Social media policy is the most important starting place for creating a school-wide and district-wide culture that embraces social media as a powerful tool for communicating, teaching, and learning. Procedures and professional development, which we will discuss in chapters 5 and 6, will transform your vision and plan from words on paper to real practices that have measurable effects on teaching, learning, and communications in your school system.

GETTING YOUR BOARD ON BOARD

As your policy language and employee guidelines come together, you will reach a point where the next logical step is adoption of these documents by the school board. Convincing school board members to accept your vision and plan can feel like a daunting task, but it is essential to the success of your social media embrace.

In Eudora, the first policy and employee guidelines were ready to be presented shortly after the internal consensus-building process was finished. In some districts, this approval or work may take place earlier in the process, before a wide range of leaders are involved. In Eudora, the superintendent worked hard to keep board members in the loop, so they were aware that this work was taking place behind the scenes. By the time the guidelines and policy language were presented to the board for approval, there was confidence that the board would consent to these items and allow the changes to continue moving forward. It should also be noted that the changes in board policy in 2014 did nothing to change this document—the guidelines adopted in 2013 have withstood review and remain in place as written.

The work you have already done to build consensus with leaders and key decision makers must now continue with board members. This is a time when it can be quite useful to come back to all the reasons why embracing the social media shift is important, and in this case, your job involves tailoring all the reasons *why* to the viewpoints, values, and priorities of your school board. You are still selling the same vision, but your target audience has changed, so your message will need to change, as well. While each local school board reflects the uniqueness of its community, the vast majority of board members are highly motivated by opportunities to improve teaching and learning, strategies to build public trust, and steps to manage risk.

Not unlike superintendents and other top executives, school board members see the operation of a district through a global lens, and for that reason, it's time to frame your recommended policies and plans around three questions that are both resonant and compelling to most school board members:

- How can we create more opportunities for students?
- How can we make sure we keep our students, staff, and district free from harm online?
- How does this build trust between district officials, families, and community members? (Remember, voters are the people who allow school board members to remain in office. Do not miss the chance to highlight how a trusting relationship between the schools and community members can ultimately maintain or build upon the board's positive reputation with voters.)

The more illustrative you can be in answering these questions, the greater the chance that board members will hear your argument in terms that inspire and motivate them. This is another great time to share any data and feedback that has been collected. How many sites did you find on social media that already represent, or give the impression of representing, your schools and/or district? How many teachers or employees are already using these tools as part of their job, but on their own? What types of communication and information do parents want from teachers, schools, and the district?

Show the yet-untapped opportunities available, and explain how the risk will be managed with policy, procedures, and professional development. Continue to genuinely acknowledge board members' fears and concerns, and listen to their questions with curiosity. Is there a way to improve the plan or policy to better address the barriers they see? This process may take one meeting, or a series of meetings. Work with your top leaders to ensure that the proposal continues to be heard with the same sense of forward momentum that's been established in your work so far.

The approval of board policy and employee guidelines is the final hurdle in your work toward implementation. Because this is such a critical time in the process, do not force it or allow it to be rushed. Take the time you need to build your messages and process around the collaboration of key stakeholders, data about social media use in society and among your district students and parents, and a clear plan for the next steps moving forward.

KEY IDEAS TO REMEMBER

- District policy for social media should outline expectations and consequences for use of the tools by employees, students, and families. It should also be realistically enforceable, acknowledging the nature of social media use. It's wise to first review existing board policies to identify areas where social media might easily fit.
- Cyberbullying is a very real concern and is taking place in nearly every school system. All districts, whether ready to embrace social media or not, should take steps now to protect students and employees from the effects of cyberbullying through policy.
- Employee guidelines, when adopted by the board of education, are valuable tools to help teachers and staff members of all ages and experience levels understand how to use social media both personally and professionally. They also provide a clear framework by which supervisors can address an employee's inappropriate use of social media.
- While working to build support among school board members, communication should be focused on the potential to create opportunities for students, manage real risk, and build trust between district officials, families, and community members.

FIVE

Procedures

Organize the Chaos

Big change is a funny thing. No matter how much passion exists around making it happen, there will be moments when the excited anticipation is replaced with emotions ranging from mild anxiety to all-out panic. During the months it took the Eudora team to move through the consensus-building process, there was so much momentum that, at times, it felt like all excitement and progress. But throughout the process, big questions did come up, from feedback groups and individuals. During these moments of uncertainty, the social media embrace quickly felt overwhelming.

A range of doubts percolated about how *on earth* it might be possible to keep track of all the details that encompassed the district's social media shift, including who would bear responsibility and accountability for making sure each of those details is addressed:

- How will we make sure everyone is trained on new employee guidelines—and how will we actually enforce the guidelines when they're in place?
- How will we know who is using social media for work, and how they are using it?
- How will we be able to monitor so many different accounts from different social media platforms, across multiple schools, departments, and locations?
- If a principal or director isn't on Facebook or another chosen social platform, how can he or she provide support and accountability for the teachers and other staff members who are?

- Whom should employees call if something uncomfortable or negative comes up as they use social media in their work, or if they are approached by a concerned parent?
- Who is responsible for following up on a report of inappropriate use of social media by an employee?
- Which students can—or cannot—have their photo or other information posted on a social media site, and how will we make sure our teachers and staff members know?

It's clear that a rapidly changing tool for communicating, teaching, and learning—particularly one that has a well-deserved reputation for risk—demands structure and organization to function both effectively and positively. As Eudora leaders moved from consensus building to implementation, it became evident that a well-defined set of procedures would be required to provide structure to the district's new socially connected environment. And it was firmly decided that these procedures would fully reflect the newly open attitude around social media.

The steps Eudora teachers and employees are asked to follow are designed to be simple, friendly, and encouraging. The essence of the procedures focuses on finding a way to share information—from teachers and staff members, to administrators, and back again. Creating these procedures involved the design of three new pieces of the social media shift puzzle: an online information-sharing form, direct support through the use of administrative privileges within social media accounts, and the establishment of social media champions in the district's schools and relevant departments.

INFORMATION-SHARING FORM

Support from administrators was one of the key concerns expressed by employees as implementation of the social media embrace continued. Looking back over the early stages of the shift, Eudora teacher Ryan Jacobs said, "I needed to know that I was going to be supported if I used social media in my classroom. There was a lot of uncertainty at the beginning, and there was no track record, yet, of how administrators would handle any questions or concerns that came up."

Administrators, on the other hand, were concerned about how they would know who was using social media, how it was being used by their employees, and what types of support employees might need. Recognizing that supervisors and employees would have distinct needs, an online form was developed to open up the lines of communication between anyone wishing to create or maintain a work-related social media account, and the administrators responsible for supervising them. While the use of such a form will vary depending on the size of a school system, three main features make this procedure effective:

Make It Short, Simple, and Painless

Without vigilant and consistent monitoring, it is all but impossible to control which employees are using social media for work. But remember: *This social media shift is about empowerment, not control.* To encourage positive participation in the district's new social media opportunities, the process for employees must be as free as possible from obstacle and burden. The fewer the hoops to jump through, and the easier those few hoops are, the more likely employees are to follow the process and — most importantly — establish themselves on the district's radar.

Embed Key Policies and Guidelines

Include direct links to the newly adopted board policy and employee guidelines to ensure that employees registering their sites or accounts clearly understand what is expected of them. This also makes the online form a familiar spot where employees can find and review these resources quickly on their own, when needed.

Create Value for the Employee

In reality, this form is more about what is needed on the administrative side than what teachers and employees inherently need to get started on social media. Because there is no reasonable way to require such a form be used, it's important to find ways that it can provide added value for those employees who take the time to follow the process. In Eudora, this led to the creation of a "social media directory" on the district website—a page prominently featured on the site and regularly shared in school newsletters and on district social media accounts.

To promote the positive engagement of parents and supporters, the social media directory is devoted to listing all the known social media accounts across our district, including Facebook pages and groups, Twitter handles, YouTube channels, blogs, and other social media accounts. (Even those accounts with higher privacy settings or available only to certain groups of parents or students are included, to give visitors the complete view of where they may be able to engage with our schools on social media.) Not only does the directory give current employees a resource for ideas and inspiration, but this type of publicity also serves as a great carrot to employees with social media accounts in the ongoing quest to build followers!

Once an employee has filled out the form and understands and agrees to the established policies and guidelines, the contents of the form are sent automatically to supervisors and the district-level communications office. (The form also is sent to social media champions, a group of teachers discussed later in this chapter.) Most forms arrive complete, which leads promptly to the account being added to the social media directory page on the district website.

Occasionally, a form will arrive incomplete, or with a question included. This is the perfect opportunity to hash through any lingering questions or concerns that the employee, or an administrator, may have. Sometimes the submitter simply wants one more reassurance that everything is set up properly before officially rolling out their new social media account.

With these three goals in mind, the resulting employee form serves as an important two-way communications tool between social media users and the administrators who support them.

DIRECT SUPPORT

One of the steps required on the information-sharing form is an agreement to establish at least one other person with administrative privileges on an account. Employees are required to give a supervisor (ideally, their principal or director) administrative privileges for Facebook pages or groups and blogs, and to provide login credentials for platforms that don't include administrative features, such as Twitter and Instagram.

When the district's social media embrace rolled out, most Eudora Schools principals did *not* personally use Facebook, so the district's communications director was included as an option for this role. In the time since, the makeup of the district's leadership team has shifted to include a much higher percentage of social media users, making administrative involvement even more streamlined and meaningful to teachers and supervisors alike.

Thinking of administrative supervision of employees' social media use certainly evokes mixed feelings, and this is an important touch point in the process of implementing these changes. Since the overarching goal of the social media shift is to encourage an embrace of these new tools, it is critical to speak about and use administrative privileges with great care and specific intention.

In no way should these privileges be used by a principal or other supervisor to micromanage or interfere with an employee's social media account. The person responsible for content and comments is, without question, the teacher who owns the account. Make no mistake: The role of a principal, director, or other supervisor with administrative privileges on a social media account is to be there when support is needed, but otherwise enjoy the owner's content and stay out of the way. However, there are occasions when the person responsible for an account is unable or unavailable to manage activity within that account; these are the times when administrative privileges are critical.

Consider this scenario: A bus full of sixth graders is involved in a traffic accident on a field trip to a nearby natural history museum. The accident is being reported in the news, and the sixth-grade teachers' social media accounts are starting to light up. Although everyone is safe on the bus, updating a Facebook page or sending a tweet is low on the list of that teacher's priorities while managing a chaotic scene and keeping students safely in check.

Now imagine this same scenario, but the crash involves critical injuries or even fatalities. If one of your teachers or employees is involved in such an incident, he or she must never be expected to communicate clearly to parents in the midst of a tragedy or crisis. In this case—or in any variety of situations that happen in school districts of all kinds, every day—having a backup account administrator is an insurance policy that school and district messages can continue to flow directly to key audiences, even when normal routines are disrupted.

Even top-level district and school accounts benefit greatly from having additional layers of administrative privileges woven in. If there's a lockdown at the middle school, someone at the district office can be updating the middle school page *as the middle school voice* while allowing the school's leadership team maximum flexibility to respond as needed to the event at hand.

Even without a crisis, the backup administrative privileges can be extremely useful in communicating important information—bus delays, canceled practices, or class schedule changes—at a time when a principal is unable to access the school's account, due to traveling, a drained phone battery, internet or power outages, or any variety of everyday obstacles.

Those added to accounts with administrative privileges also will have a first-row seat to the interactions that are taking place in a social media community. Notifications generated to account administrators through the social media sites themselves make it quite simple for principals and directors to have a sense of the interactions taking place on a variety of pages every day.

SOCIAL MEDIA CHAMPIONS

While the online information-sharing form resolved many of Eudora leaders' questions about managing the creation and growth of multiple independent social media accounts, a form is a poor substitute for providing real support to employees. Considering the emerging plan and the consensus that was being built, it became clear that *people* would be needed in order to make a real difference in encouraging and supporting district employees. This need for a network of connected and engaged employees led to the development of a group of *social media champions*. With a bit of additional social media training and guidance provided by the school district, these teacher leaders provide guidance and basic technical support for their colleagues on an as-needed, ongoing basis throughout the school year.

The discussion of social media champions should include a note about the ideal person to serve in this role. As a small district with limited resources, there weren't teachers or other employees in Eudora whose existing positions encompassed this type of work. Over the years, those serving as social media champions have been people without special designation or responsibility for technology mentoring.

But consider this caveat for districts or schools where these positions may already exist: Social media leadership tends to be specific to the person, much more so than the job title. A "regular" teacher who is personally interested in and energized by using social media in schools may be just as likely—or in some cases more likely—to be an effective social media champion than a technology teacher or instructional technologist. The work to create a group of social media champions must focus on finding the individuals who best fit the champion role, with much less emphasis on a person's job title or content area.

In a small school system, it is very manageable to gather all of the district's social media champions together for the occasional meeting. A larger district could certainly meet in the district-wide group, but breaking champions out among grade levels could also be extremely useful. For example, the way that primary grade level teachers use social media for teaching, learning, and communication will differ wildly from the way that middle or high school teachers use it. In a district with many social media champions across dozens of schools and campuses, meetings in smaller groups that reflect narrower grade groupings could be a meaningful solution.

The role of social media champions has evolved over time. Champions have always received the information-sharing forms that are submitted when an employee is setting up a new social media account. From there, they follow up with the colleagues who submitted the forms and touch base throughout the year to offer encouragement and support, as well as to share information or exchange ideas.

The role of the champions has also grown to include making sure the social media directory is kept up to date. At least once a year, the volunteer leaders reach out to the people in their building whose accounts are listed on the directory. This has been an effective way to clean up old or inactive accounts, as well as to become aware of teachers or other staff members who need to fill out an information-sharing form so that their existing social media account can be added to the online directory.

"In the role of social media champion, I am always available to help anyone that is just starting out on the social media path," said Niki Rheuport, fifth-grade teacher and social media champion at Eudora Elementary School. "I reassure anyone who might be as reluctant as I was, and I always learn something new from the teachers I speak with who use social media or are just starting out on it. With the ever-evolving world of social media, we must learn from each other and be open to leaving our comfort zone in order to stay up-to-date."

Once the social media shift has begun, there must be an ongoing commitment to providing professional development to all employees, including additional levels of contact to help prepare champions to serve in their role. Professional development will be discussed more thoroughly in the next chapter, but education leaders should consider any number of ongoing communications tools to keep their social media champions engaged on a regular basis.

In Eudora, there is a private Facebook group limited only to the current champions for sharing updates, asking questions, and discussing available resources; a blog, wiki, or other online collaboration tools also could be useful. Whatever tool is used, the primary focus should be to keep social media champions connected with one another over time. Keep in mind, however, that the most powerful opportunity for social media champions to connect and collaborate is when they are given time to meet and share ideas, at least once a year.

COMMENTS AND RESPONSES

The final area of procedure in a social media shift deals directly with one of the things that educators and education leaders are likely to fear most: negative comments. The first step in overcoming this fear is to acknowledge that the worst part about 99 percent of negative comments is just that they make you feel bad. That's right: When someone says something negative or nasty about your schools, your employees, or your students, you don't like it.

But often, when you look at a negative comment with that in mind and set your emotional response aside, the steps to take can become obvious and uncomplicated. However, it's one thing for an owner of a social media account to see a clear path, but that may not entirely put to rest the hurt and anxiety of those who are paying attention, including principals, directors, superintendents, or school board members. Having a clear response procedure in place pays dividends when leaders or co-workers ask such questions as, "How are you going to respond to *that*?" or "Aren't you going to do something about that?"

It's important to remember at this point that it actually doesn't matter if a school system has even begun to embrace the social media shift — negative comments are already being posted for the world to see, whether on the social media accounts of parents, employees, or community members, or simply on the comments sections of the stories posted by the local media outlet. An awareness of these comments is an important first step, but a systematized way of handling them is what empowers you to protect your district's reputation without spending time rushing around to put out every fire. An organized approach for responding to social media comments will be discussed in chapter 10.

Procedures connect all the dots around the embrace of social media, making your policy work for teachers, staff members, and administrators. Procedures also define the roles and responsibilities for the work that has to happen. The investment of time to lay these out and create the online or paper forms needed will position district leaders and staff members to work as thoughtfully and professionally as possible in the new social media environment.

KEY IDEAS TO REMEMBER

- With so many moving parts, the key to a successful embrace of social media is developing procedures that share important account information and facilitate accountability.
- All procedures must be designed to be simple and encouraging; those that offer an incentive of some kind, such as being listed in a school-wide or district-wide social media directory, will be most successful.
- Purposeful sharing of administrative privileges on social media accounts can provide direct support to employees when they need it most. Supervisors should never use these privileges to interfere with or micromanage a responsible employee's appropriate social media use.
- Recruiting and training a group of social media champions in each building and/or from each collaborative team is an effective way to provide routine support and encouragement for social media users in a school system.
- A clear process should be established and shared describing how negative or untrue comments or posts should be handled.

SIX

Professional Development

Educate and Empower

Professional development is the third and final area of a framework that allows education leaders to embrace and implement the social media shift while managing the risk inherent in it. Professional development is nothing short of a necessity, given the new policies and procedures that have been adopted. And as professional development activities are designed and planned, it is critical to continue to focus on encouraging and supporting district employees in their use of social media, just as was done when policies and procedures were being written.

This chapter will address both the professional development that administrators must provide to employees, as well as the rich opportunities afforded to educators willing to use social media for their own, customized professional learning and growth.

STARTING OUT RIGHT

Bus driver training is largely dedicated to understanding the everyday hazards involved with driving a bus full of children and teenagers on busy streets. Likewise, the first goal of training employees about the use of social media is simple: Understand the risks. There are, of course, two ways to go about this. One way is to scare employees about the dangers of social media. While effective at communicating the dangers embedded in social media, the vast majority of educators (and employees in general) are deeply motivated by job security and risk avoidance. For that reason, a "scared straight" approach will result in most employees deciding to steer clear and avoid the risks altogether. By now, you should recognize that your goal is the converse of this approach. Instead of scaring your employees away from social media, describe the risks in a way that helps them understand and manage them, while simultaneously embracing the unique and exciting opportunities offered.

In Eudora, the new social media policies and procedures were developed and adopted in the spring, following several months of dedicated work. With the end of the school year approaching and just one remaining in-service day for teachers before summer, time was set aside to provide an informational training to our employees about the new policies and procedures that had been adopted—and would be in place when they returned in the fall.

Eudora consultant Ben Smith agreed to provide these one-hour sessions to groups of fifty to one hundred staff members at a time. To ensure that each district employee was well aware of the newly articulated expectations about social media, his presentation began with a brief but thorough review of the new employee guidelines that had been adopted by the school board. These expectations—which, if you remember, were first requested by the local teachers' association president—defined a new set of standards for employee behavior online. It was critical that professionals in the school system understood that these guidelines applied both at work and in their personal use of social media—and that their continued employment depended on their understanding of and adherence to these newly outlined expectations.

However, the presentation of the guidelines was immediately followed up with a dynamic and engaging presentation about why social media is so important to communication, teaching, and learning in today's world. Most importantly, Smith concluded each presentation by highlighting many of the tools available to educators, as well as the enormous benefits that can be enjoyed by teachers and other staff members through the use of social media in their work. (Certainly, this information and training could be presented to larger groups, or the presentation could be recorded and provided to employees electronically.)

"It's so important for teachers and other employees to understand the risks, but for those risks to be presented in a way that they are manageable, not scary," Smith later reflected. "Spending the majority of the time talking about the need to embrace social media and the opportunities that exist when you do—that's how you keep the process moving forward and gain more support and buy-in over time."

THE DIGITAL TATTOO

One of the most important messages that people—in particular those working in a school system—must understand is that their lives on social media are public, and they are permanent. Despite the common perception about privacy settings, they are not a guarantee of privacy, especially on social media, which is built for the express purpose of sharing content with other people. (Even someone with a high desire for privacy on Facebook still opens an account to share information with at least one other person.)

On Facebook alone, there are many ways that a post intended to be private can become public, from someone screen capturing and reposting or copying and pasting the post on their own, less private, account. There are countless examples of someone inadvertently changing the audience to public when posting a photo or update. Just as in sharing sensitive information in a crowded restaurant, it can never be fully guaranteed that shared information will not be picked up—and passed on—by someone else.

Similarly, there is a common misconception that posts to social media are not permanent, especially if they can be deleted later. In fact, posts to social media are far more permanent than they appear to the average user. Because content can be shared beyond the original post through the use of screenshots or simple copy and paste, permanence is always a possibility.

A rant posted by a teacher about his or her principal may only have been shared with a few close friends and then deleted a short while later when better judgment prevailed. However, if in those few hours, or even minutes or seconds, before deleting, someone copied and pasted it, or otherwise shared it with even one other person, the deleted post still remains.

The other consideration in the question of permanence is the fact that all updates, photos, and videos posted in any public online space are indexed by Google and other search engines for hours, days, or even a few weeks. This very thing was illustrated to district leaders in Eudora when a former teacher who had been arrested on a Friday night promptly deactivated a suite of personal social media accounts, including a blog and profiles on both LinkedIn and Facebook. Well into the week following the arrest, the information from these accounts—including some photos and posts—were still available in search engine previews, even though the teacher's actual sites were unavailable.

Because the people who work in schools are human beings—and all human beings make mistakes—it's important for education leaders to take time with employees to introduce and talk about the idea of a digital tattoo. Like a tattoo, posts on social media make a statement about who you are, they are typically visible to the public, and they are very difficult, if not sometimes impossible, to completely erase. Providing this insight will allow every employee in the school system—from the twenty-two-year-old recent college graduate to the fifty-two-year-old veteran teacher—the chance to reflect on the public and permanent nature of their lives on social media.

This discussion also drives home for individuals, in a concrete and eye-opening way, how important prudence and mindfulness are when sharing information and content on social media, especially in an emotional moment where there is a measurable and often strong psychological impulse to click "post" or "tweet." It also begins to equip employees with the knowledge and mindset to help mentor students as digital citizens, giving teachers and other staff members a powerful perspective to share with the young people they work with each day.

ONGOING SUPPORT

With new policies and guidelines in place, and the first step of professional development needs met, the next step is to identify meaningful opportunities for continued training over the following months and years. Here are a few ways to ensure that people continue to learn about—and be reminded of—the employee guidelines, expectations, and opportunities as staff teams shift and change over time.

Training New Teachers

Summer induction programs are the perfect time to orient new teachers in the district to your social media expectations and opportunities. The most intensive ongoing training effort within Eudora Schools takes place as new employees go through orientation and induction each August. The social media session is typically presented in an hour or less by the communications director or other appropriate administrator, with about one-third of the time spent on guidelines and policies and two-thirds spent exploring opportunities and encouraging new team members to give it a try.

Annual Reminders to All Employees

Once an employee has received the basic introduction to the social media policies, guidelines, and expectations, these items should be reviewed annually. This works well when it is embedded in the back-to-school meetings planned by principals, but friendly reminders also may be provided to all employees through mass emails, handbook reviews, or mailbox fliers.

Occasional In-Service

When in-service day agendas are planned, they might include sessions for employees seeking more guidance, support, or information about social media in their jobs. These tend to be smaller groups that review a few basic points before opening up to a group discussion. This discussion can be structured or unstructured, guided or free, depending on the goals of the group. It also should include time for troubleshooting any issues that employees may be having with their use of social networks.

Short sessions of an hour or less also work well for those teachers or other staff members who want hands-on guidance as they choose which type of social media tool is best for their needs and make the privacy settings work for them.

Informal Discussion Groups

Outside of formal in-service days, similar small groups also can be assembled before or after school, or during planning or collaboration periods, by individual groups of teachers or staff members. These small, unstructured groups provide a format for deeper discussions around specific tools, answering such questions as, "What's the difference between a Facebook page and a Facebook group, and which is right for me?" or "How would I best use social media to help me reach X objective?" It is always rewarding to meet with these teachers to encourage and support them as they embrace the social media shift for themselves.

Social Media Champions

Social media champions, as described in chapter 5, provide invaluable ongoing professional development in their building, whether with groups of colleagues or individuals, as needed.

STUDENT PRIVACY

Throughout the work of embracing the social media shift in schools, it is normal for concerns of privacy and confidentiality to come up. Protecting the privacy of student data is a top priority in a wide range of school operations, both because it's the right thing to do and because it's mandated by federal law.

Since the 1970s, the Family Education Rights and Privacy Act (FERPA) has protected the educational records of students and given parents of students under eighteen some control over the disclosure of information from school records. Until the late 1990s and early 2000s, it's reasonable to assume that this law dealt most directly with release of student information to college and military recruiters, as well as local newspaper reporters. But with the advent of the internet and, more recently, the sharing world of social media, education leaders have had to seriously reexamine the expectations that students and parents have about the release of information in an interconnected digital age.

The FERPA procedures in Eudora have not undergone major changes as a result of the social media embrace; however, "video images" and "audio recordings" were added to the list of designated directory information, in addition to the more traditional name, address, and photograph. "School district website and official social media sites" are both provided as examples of how the district might use a student's directory information.

By adding these two types of content as directory information and disclosing the website and social media purpose, the district's right to release student information on social media has been clearly established, unless the parent opts out. Because Eudora is a small district, the FERPA opt-out list is managed centrally in a cloud document and shared to all district employees so that any teacher, secretary, or coach can tell, at a glance, if a student in their class, team, or club is allowed to be featured on social media.

In the vast majority of cases, teachers and staff should be discouraged from creating additional consent procedures specific to social media; if they are covered in FERPA, consistency in practice and compliance is ensured across the school system. Classroom-level consenting also creates confusion from parents who then may get the impression that other teachers are not following protocol when they rely on the FERPA disclosure list.

But, as with all things, having the right to do something doesn't always make it the right thing to do. For that reason, professional development opportunities also are used as opportunities to discuss with teachers and staff members the best ways to share information about students on social media. Here are a few of the best practices that have been adopted across the district:

- Check the opt-out list on a regular basis to know which students in your classroom or on your team should not be pictured on social media.
- Disable any feature that allows others to "tag" themselves or others in your photos or posts. While it seems harmless, allowing others to tag photos or posts can create privacy concerns for students and families that are otherwise best avoided. Encourage parents to use the "sharing" feature for a favorite photo or post that they want their friends and followers to see.
- When posting to a public account about the district's youngest students, consider photographing classroom activities without directly showing students' faces. There are easy ways to highlight classroom projects, such as by standing behind a student working at a desk. Posting a photograph of many students together also tends to be less uncomfortable to many parents than posting a close-up of one child's face.

- For most social media posts, if any student name is used, use a first name only. One exception would be a post about a specific student who has been honored with an award or other special recognition.
- If in doubt, ask permission. If there's a costume day, a silly skit, or a blooper reel from a sports practice, ask yourself if the students involved, or their parents, could be embarrassed. If that possibility exists, it's always best to ask before you post.
- Be reasonable if a parent or student asks you to remove a post on social media. In Eudora, this has happened only a handful of times over several years; in each case, there was a legitimate (and genuinely inadvertent) concern that was easily addressed by simply editing the post. Don't assume that a concern means a post must be removed—often there are compromises that can satisfy all parties without too much sacrifice.

MONITORING ACCOUNTS

One of the reasons why many Eudora teachers and employees quickly adopted the use of social media for their work is because it felt so natural. Those employees who were already familiar with one or more social networks found the learning curve to be very manageable. And for the vast majority of these employees, monitoring their new school-focused social media account became a natural extension of their existing use.

For those who are already using Facebook, for example, it takes very little effort to also post to the classroom page or group, and the ease of posting with smartphones makes this even simpler. "I will take a photo or short video of kids working on a project in the classroom and can post it to our class Instagram and Facebook group within just a couple of minutes as they're working," said Eudora Middle School social studies teacher Ryan Jacobs.

But regular updates are required for social media to be effective— frequent posts are much more likely to be seen by followers, and the number of followers is far more likely to grow for an account with dynamic content. For that reason, it's important that all employees using social media for work understand the expectations for monitoring their school social media accounts. Some basic expectations to consider are:

- If a page or group is set up, the responsible teacher or employee will post some kind of update at least once a week. (This can be as easy as sharing a post from another account, posting the week's lunch menu, or posting a quick photo of student artwork or chalkboard writing straight from a smartphone.)
- The responsible teacher will respond to any post from a parent or student—either on the social media page, with a phone call or email

message, or in person—within twenty-four to forty-eight hours, including during weekends and breaks.

- Negative or uncomfortable posts or comments will be handled according to the response guidelines (see chapter 10), with support as needed from a social media champion and/or supervisor.
- Breaks from school are a great time to keep social media content flowing and keep students and parents engaged. But if there will be a significant gap of time between posts, such as during summer break or over an extended medical leave, the teacher will post a message before break to explain. "Have a great summer, keep reading, and we'll see you next year!" is a simple way to make sure a lapse in posts doesn't make an account look ignored or forgotten.
- If a teacher or other employee responsible for a social media account resigns or otherwise decides to stop using social media, that person must deactivate the account and notify the appropriate supervisor so that the page can be removed from the district's social media directory. If the group or account will be maintained by a different employee, full administrative privileges and login credentials will be given to a supervisor to ensure a smooth transition. It is wise to include these procedures and expectations as part of the standard checkout process when an employee leaves the district.

RECOGNIZE TO ENCOURAGE

Key to encouraging teachers to adopt social media as a classroom tool is recognizing those who are willing to try. By showcasing the ways that local teachers are using social media effectively, you simultaneously give a pat on the back to those who were willing to take the (measured) risk and shine a light on the work that you hope to see from others.

Greg Turchetta is executive director of communications and community engagement for Collier County Public Schools in Naples, Florida. When he launched a campaign to get district teachers on Twitter, he devised a way to reward them for their willingness to do something different with #Tweetcher designation. "As we rolled out this initiative in nearly fifty schools," Turchetta said, "we knew that recognition is something educators often try to avoid. However, in the social media space, recognition is a critical component to classroom adoption. If you are going to ask teachers to add another task to their already overbooked day, they must see the value, and their innovative efforts must be celebrated."

The superintendent of Collier County Schools, Dr. Kamela Patton, made a point to celebrate social media success, and challenged the principals at schools with lower adoption rates to encourage more use. "#Tweetchers truly appreciate principal praise and peer to peer acknowledgment of their social media creativity in the classroom," Turchetta said. "We also worked to share best practices and awarded schools with a traveling award called "Where It's @."

The leadership efforts were so well received that the district developed additional recognition and awards for teachers who model exceptional use of social media in the classroom. A rubber bracelet imprinted with #tweetcher and the district logo has become a visual marker of social media adoption across the district. The first bracelets were hand-delivered to star performers in their classrooms. "The visit and the praise mattered much more than the nineteen-cent bracelet," Turchetta said. "The kids always asked to take a class picture with the award and then asked their teacher to tweet it out! We have since given a bag of #tweetcher bracelets to each principal to give any teachers that tweet for their class."

Turchetta added, "The recognition definitely helped grow our social media effort. However, the biggest piece to encouraging continued social media use is the retweet button. Sharing the best classroom content each day validates their efforts. It reinforces that this is worth sharing at the classroom, school, and district level. If you do nothing else, retweet their content, each and every day."

EXPAND THE PLN

Apart from the professional development that education leaders should provide to their employees, social media itself offers tremendous opportunities for teachers and other staff members to network, learn, and grow as professionals.

Andrew Maxey, director of special programs for Tuscaloosa City Schools in Alabama, is passionate about the value Twitter offers any education professional for learning and growth. "If we were allowed one reason, most educators would say we're on Twitter to connect with, and learn from, others. Twitter is rightly called the world's largest PLN—or faculty workroom. I interact with educators on other social media platforms, but Twitter interactions exceed all other social media interactions combined."

He added, "It is also very accessible because the norms of Twitter make it perfectly fine for a teacher to lurk and learn at first. Chats tend to value the voice of all participants for what they contribute—making credentials irrelevant. Other platforms don't seem to nurture growth of new folks in the same way."

Amanda Spight, an elementary principal in Belton, Missouri, credits Twitter chats with much of her professional growth, and encourages her teachers to take advantage, as well. "For me, the most significant benefit of Twitter," Spight said, "has been the opportunity to engage in conversation with leading experts in the field. I have had many conversations with (author) Todd Whitaker in Twitter chats, for example. I also enjoy just being able to see how different building and district leaders implement initiatives."

Twitter chats have been essential for Spight, something that she shares with teachers in her building. After narrowing down the chats to the half dozen she finds most meaningful—including #KidsDeserveIt, #LeadLAP, #CultureEd, and #K12PRchat—she takes every opportunity to invite others in her school to join, as well as when she works with new and aspiring administrators.

And while chats are a powerful way to connect participants with colleagues around the world, the value also can be concentrated within a single school community. One school in Wisconsin's Howard-Suamico School District has shifted one staff meeting a year to Twitter. Communications coordinator Brian Nicol explained, "The leadership team at Bay View Middle School 'flipped' staff meetings by moving preparation ahead of the meeting time, leaving meetings open for collaboration and learning. The natural extension of that approach was to flex one meeting a year into a Twitter-chat format."

The potential for individual educators to grow as professionals through the use of social media tools—in particular through Twitter and blogs—is so great that it can be overwhelming, especially for those who are not entirely comfortable with the platforms themselves. Fortunately, there is no shortage of resources available to orient a novice to the exciting online tools available for professional development. Start with a simple Google search for such terms as *Twitter for teachers*, or just strike up a conversation with someone in your building or district who is already enjoying the benefits of professional connectivity on social media. So often, the most daunting step is the first one—once you take that first step, the benefits and advantages will be well worth your time and investment.

These last three chapters have covered the practical steps for education leaders to follow to bring about an embrace of the social media shift within a school system. Policies, procedures, and professional development work together to effectively manage the risk of this shift. The next chapters will focus on specific strategies and uses that will allow your district or school to leverage social media as an indispensable tool for teaching, learning, and communicating.

KEY IDEAS TO REMEMBER

- Professional development for employees should be focused on educating and encouraging—not scaring. Teaching employees about the risks of social media use is critical, but it must be done in a way that empowers them to use the tools for good.

- An essential part of professional development for all employees is a discussion of the "digital tattoo," or the fact that everything posted to any social network should be considered both *public* and *permanent.*
- All new employees should receive training on the expectations and consequences surrounding social media use, as outlined in the board-approved employee guidelines. An ongoing combination of in-service sessions and informal small-group meetings can provide refreshers and guided work time for employees using social media in their job. Social media champions are another excellent resource for day-to-day, personal support of those using social media at work.
- All employees must understand expectations surrounding student privacy and confidentiality, as much in the digital world as in every other part of school district operations.
- Employees using social media for work should be expected to monitor their accounts at all times, including weekends and school breaks.
- Recognizing teachers and staff who are successfully using social media is one of the simplest ways to reinforce best practices and inspire employees to take chances and try new things. Traveling trophies and small tokens of recognition can encourage participation and pride in the innovation, but the biggest priority should be to highlight teachers' great content publicly—through retweets and other social shares.
- Social media can be a powerful tool for educators to expand their own learning and professional growth. Encouraging teachers to take advantage of these free and easily accessed tools can have a positive, tangible effect on a school's professional culture.

SEVEN

Social Media Best Practices

Think of *Mork and Mindy*, the classic (and quirky) sitcom from the late 1970s and early 1980s. In the series, Robin Williams played Mork, an alien who arrived on Earth in a one-man egg-shaped space ship. The storylines—and comedic success—of the show revolved around Mork's efforts to understand human behavior and American culture, including a wide range of misunderstandings that frustrated and sometimes offended his human friend and roommate, Mindy.

The ever-shifting world of social media is hardly a foreign planet, but many of the fears and frustrations surrounding it are based on the fact that it is a new, perhaps slightly even alien-feeling, type of social structure. And when you think about social media not just as a tool—but also as a dynamic and constantly evolving community of people—it becomes clear that a social media embrace will only be effective when education leaders recognize and follow the community norms. Just as you seek to understand your local community and groups of stakeholders *IRL* (In Real Life), your success using social media depends on learning about and respecting the norms of interaction and behavior in the digital world.

Certainly, anyone who already has a personal Facebook page, Instagram account, or other social media profile already understands a great deal of the expectations of the social media community. However, it takes far more than personal use of social media to understand how to best harness its potential as a positive force in a school system.

WRITING YOUR POST

The first, and very often overlooked, rule is to respect the "social" of social media. When is the last time you heard a friend or family member begin a conversation with the words *Please note, Administration has an-*

nounced, or *It has come to our attention*? Odds are, the people you spend time with don't typically begin their conversations in such a sterile, impersonal manner. The best part of working in school systems is the fact that the work revolves around helping people.

Every day, education leaders are helping students and families, and a major part of this work is built on communicating with kindness and humanity. These same strategies must carry over to our messages on social media. To reach your audience, posts on social media must be social and human, not administrative and robotic. Here are a few examples that illustrate how even the most mundane message can easily become more social:

- UNSOCIAL: Please note: Today is the deadline for Kindergarten Roundup packets. The school office will be open until 6:30.
- SOCIAL: Calling all 2018–2019 kindergarten families . . . today's the day! Stop by any time before 6:30 this evening to pick up your Kindergarten Roundup packet. Click the link for all the details — and WELCOME future [insert mascot name, e.g., Cardinals]!

- UNSOCIAL: The Board of Education voted last night to approve a new attendance calendar with additional student attendance days on May 15 and 16. These days were required to meet state-mandated attendance hours following an excess of inclement weather days. Click the link for an updated copy.
- SOCIAL: Calendar update! Last night, our Board of Education approved an updated May calendar to make up days after such a cold, snowy winter. Click the link to download your new copy.

- UNSOCIAL: Graduates must report no later than 10:30 a.m. on Thursday for the required graduation practice. No exceptions!
- SOCIAL: Attention Class of 2019 — make sure you're on time for graduation practice this Thursday at 10:30 a.m. so you are ready to enjoy your special day. If you can't make it, be sure to talk to Mrs. Jackson today!

- UNSOCIAL: Important announcement: The drop-off procedures at school have changed, due to major traffic issues. Cars must pull up to the drop-off zone before letting students out of cars, and no child will be allowed in the building before 7:30 a.m. — Administration
- SOCIAL: We need your help! Please click the link to review new drop-off procedures that are designed to help keep your student

and family safe during the busy morning run. Call the office if you have questions, and THANKS for your support!

There are countless simple ways to take a dry, curt message and turn it into something that communicates the same information in a way that is human, friendly, and engaging. Not only will this type of message better fit the norms of social networks, but it also reflects the way that administrators, teachers, and staff members typically want to communicate with their students, families, and patrons.

Here is a good rule of thumb: Before you post anything, read it aloud to yourself. If it doesn't sound like the way you would talk to your friend, your neighbor, or your family, keep working on it before clicking "post."

WHAT'S A HASHTAG?

To the uninitiated, one of the more mysterious ideas is the hashtag, a search or grouping tool that originated on Twitter but has since spread to Instagram, Facebook, Pinterest, and beyond. Simply put, hashtags are short terms preceded by the pound sign (#)—for example, #education—and they have become an integral piece of how messages and information are shared online. On Twitter, the pound, or hash, sign turns any word or group of words that directly follows it into a searchable link, allowing users to track related content and conversations.

In more concrete terms, picture yourself at a major national education conference with 1,500 people in attendance. Breakfast is served in a large hotel ballroom, and around the room there are tables set up with discussion topics—flipped classroom, ESOL, mentoring new teachers, social-emotional learning, bullying, and dozens of others. You find the table with a topic that interests you, and you sit down to have a conversation with peers who share your interest.

Those discussions are exactly how hashtags work. But instead of the ballroom with everyone in one geographic place, the hashtag allows users—from around the world, and around the clock—to connect with one another around a common discussion topic, designated with a hashtag. Interested in flipped classrooms? Look up #flipclass. Science education? #scichat. Looking for new ways to use iPads for teaching? #iPaded.

An internet search for *education hashtags* will reveal hundreds of existing terms that are being used in Twitter discussions right now. And sending a tweet that includes one or more existing hashtags is the online equivalent of sitting down at that table in the ballroom—it allows you to join an ongoing conversation about the very topics that interest you, with colleagues around the globe who share your interests.

Chapter 8 includes further discussion about how classroom teachers and district leaders can leverage the power of hashtags to improve engagement for communication, teaching, and learning.

MAKE SURE YOUR MESSAGE GETS THROUGH

For most people, trying to get information from a social media newsfeed is like trying to get a drink from a fire hydrant. Some days, the Facebook feed and Twitter timeline fill up so quickly that the message you're trying to share will be lost completely in a matter of hours, or even minutes. There are specific, strategic things you can do to increase the likelihood of your message cutting through all the social media noise:

Give Your Followers What They Want

Regardless of the platform, the content you share on social media will engage your followers if it serves them the content they want. Generating great content is as simple as planning your messages around any of these five areas: (1) people they know, (2) places they love, (3) information that affects them, (4) truth in the midst of rumor, and (5) calm leadership. When your content hits on one or more of these areas, your followers will engage.

Use Photos and Video

Far and away, the posts that generate the most engagement (clicks, comments, likes or favorites, and shares or retweets) feature a compelling photo or a short video that your fans or followers enjoy. This could be a kindergarten class doing a Zumba routine in P.E., students dropping eggs or shooting off rockets in science class, highlight clips from sports teams, local news segments, or even short lectures or student presentations.

Photos are an especially effective and practical way to breathe life into a text-only post. Try including a picture of a health or P.E. classroom with a post announcing that the district's new health curriculum was approved. Liven up a post about severe weather procedures by pairing the information with a photo of storm clouds rolling in. Sign-up deadline for the Parents as Teachers program? Find a stock photo of an infant or toddler. Great news about your community? Use a photo of Main Street, an iconic local scene, or the Welcome sign displayed on a highly traveled road into town.

Education leaders managing top-level school or district accounts should build a collection of stock photography for those familiar messages that come around every year. Take photos around the schools and community as you go about your routine. The most common things — school entry signs, a bank of lockers, the lunch serving line, a morning drop-off routine, loading buses at the end of the day — can quickly take a basic post from forgettable to engaging.

Supplement local photos with high-quality stock photography from one of the many online collections, such as www.morguefile.com. These resources can be a great way to find generic photos of everything from cell phones and crayons to weather events and nature scenes.

Link to Content

Better than a text-only post, links to your website or another trusted site can add value for your audience—and engagement with your follow-ers. Social media is one of the most effective ways to increase traffic to your website, or to encourage your fans to read or learn more about important information on another trusted site, such as the local news channel, local public safety department, or helpful government agency.

Share your link in a way that motivates your audience member to click; for example, "Make sure you and your family are ready for severe weather by reviewing these tips," or "Check out everything you need to know about the finals week schedule." If you're linking to an electronic newsletter, include a headline or two in the link. Instead of "Click here for the latest newsletter," try "Field trip photos, volunteer opportunities and much more are included in the latest school newsletter—click here to read more!"

Monitor Trends

Watch for—and take advantage of—social media content trends. Throwback Thursday (also known as #ThrowbackThursday and #tbt) is one example of a recurring content theme that is very easy for school systems to participate in. Supporters of schools typically love to see photos of former school buildings, long-ago field trips, retired teachers and principals, and other blasts from the past.

If Throwback Thursday isn't a good fit for your goals, come up with your own recurring content theme. Saturday Standards were developed when Eudora Schools leaders were first communicating with parents and patrons about implementation of Common Core standards. On the first Saturday of each month, a photo was posted on the district Facebook page that showed students engaged in a learning activity directly tied to the new standards.

Over the course of more than a year, followers of the page saw middle school students writing public service announcements, high school math students outside in the cold learning about wind chill calculations, first graders using small blocks to understand that 8 + 6 is the same as 8 + 4 + 2, fifth graders compiling statistics during a March Madness basketball game, and many more examples of Eudora students benefiting from the new curriculum standards.

Also important to making sure your message gets through to your audience is your understanding of how the flow of information works within different social media platforms.

Facebook Algorithms

While the details of how Facebook decides what appears in a user's news feed are always shifting, there is one thing that you can bet on: The more a person interacts with your posts, the more often your future posts will appear in his or her feed. Your job, then, is to post content that will consistently encourage clicks, comments, shares, and likes. Facebook algorithms treat "native" posts with higher priority than posts that are being generated from an external application, such as Hootsuite, Mail-Chimp, or most other social media platforms.

The rate of content sharing by a page makes a difference, too. The ideal frequency of posting is in the neighborhood of twice a day, but at a minimum pages should include no fewer than two or three posts each week to ensure that the messages remain visible in your fans' feeds. One thing to note about Facebook is that a high-quality post can easily "live" in the social media stream for twenty-four hours, sometimes even longer. Because of the way Facebook illustrates the "like" and "comment" feature between friends, a great post from eight o'clock on Tuesday morning may still be generating clicks at lunchtime on Wednesday. By contrast, a post that doesn't generate a lot of clicks or comments in the first few hours is likely to die out of the stream fairly quickly.

Twitter

Message by message, Twitter moves at a much faster pace for users than Facebook. It's not uncommon for an average Twitter user to see hundreds of tweets per hour, as compared to perhaps a few dozen Facebook updates in the same time period. For this reason, successful message sharing on Twitter relies on repetition. If you want to tweet a revised bus schedule or news of the championship chess team, plan to tweet that message multiple times throughout the course of at least forty-eight to seventy-two hours. For this reason, Twitter better lends itself to using an external application, such as Tweetdeck or Buffer, which allow you to set up multiple tweets that can be scheduled around the clock with the hopes of showing up in your follower's timeline at the right time. (Slightly rephrasing the tweet each time helps you grab attention, rather than appearing to be a robot.)

There is one key management difference between Twitter and Facebook: Unlike Facebook, Twitter publishes tweets in the same manner and level of priority, regardless of whether they were created from the native application or an outside application. Twitter has added an algorithm, as well, to help ensure users see at least a few tweets from the people they most often interact with. These nonsequential tweets are designated as *In Case You Missed It,* ensuring that users understand these tweets are likely less recent than the other tweets in their feed. (One more reason to create content that prompts your followers' interaction is to help your tweets show up in their *In Case You Missed It* feature!)

Instagram

With a heavy emphasis on aesthetic, rather than text, Instagram is a sharing site for photos and short videos that encourages the use of creative editing and filters. Users' Instagram feeds typically move at a pace more similar to Facebook than Twitter. In most cases, posting one photo on Instagram will reach far more followers than tweeting the same photo one time. In 2017, Instagram changed from a chronological display to an algorithmic display, meaning that users will see first—and most frequently—the content posted by accounts they most often click.

YouTube

A platform that exclusively shares video content, YouTube provides an outlet for longer videos that can showcase people, programs, and events in your school system. YouTube has a well-established social fan base, giving users the ability to comment and like videos, as well as subscribe to favorite content creators and "channels." Subscribers can request email alerts each time a new video is posted.

Although YouTube is a powerful platform for video sharing, it is usually best to also upload the same video directly to Facebook, rather than posting a link on Facebook to your YouTube video. Posting the same video in two places will expand your reach; posting it native to both platforms will improve your engagement and reach, as well.

Live Video

Between 2015 and 2016, live video earned a permanent place in the social media landscape, and for good reason. If video is the most engaging content on social media, consider the additional element of surprise that is inherent in an unedited, real-time broadcast.

For school systems, live video offers an even bigger opportunity to showcase the things happening inside classrooms and buildings. From pep rallies and special announcements, to science fairs and prize patrols, education leaders now can offer families and community members outside the school walls a *real-time* look inside the dynamic, supportive learning environments they seek to create each day.

A live video from a classroom—even on the most routine day—allows a parent to be a fly on the wall, to have a front-row view of how their child's day feels. The uses for live video are as big as an educator's creativity, especially when parent and/or community engagement is a strategic goal. Consider the parent who can't make it to the special science presentation at 2 p.m. on Tuesday, or the choir concert at 7 p.m. on Thursday. If the parent can get an internet connection, live video can provide that parent a priceless view. We will take a closer look at the power of live video for communication in chapter 9.

While Facebook has become the most popular space to share live videos, Instagram, Twitter, and YouTube also offer varying degrees of live video capability. Consider these guidelines and tips when using live video in a school district setting:

- Ensure that you have the policies and procedures in place to manage the risks of social media engagement, and consider the professional development needed to help equip your teachers to successfully use live video.
- Legal restrictions for performances still apply with live video. Whether it's a second-grade music concert or a high school dance team performance, the vast majority of popular songs are protected by copyright law.
- When sharing a live video on social media, perfection is not the goal. But the quality of your video does make a difference. If possible, use a tripod (or a gimbal, if you will be moving while filming) to stabilize the video. Using an external microphone, rather than your phone's built-in mic, will greatly improve your audio.
- Plan and practice. Don't wait until the big moment to learn how to work the live stream process. If you've never used your device's live video feature before, test it out on a personal account before using it on your school or district account.
- Like any other Facebook post, live video will archive to your page, group, or event. You may only have half a dozen live viewers, but your views and engagement will balloon over the next few hours. Not only will Facebook notify your followers when you begin a live broadcast, but that video will likely rank well in news feeds for the next several hours, or longer.

Before starting a live broadcast, keep in mind that you will require a strong wireless or cellular signal on your device. For an award presentation or other special event, it is wise to plan ahead to avoid disappointment. Visit the place where the video will be broadcast and check out your cellular bars and wireless signal; consider a private hot spot if you are concerned about signal strength. And as you begin, remember that you can always switch to a separate camera, or the camera on your device, and record traditional video to upload later. It is always better to capture a special moment on standard video and share it on your social feeds than to miss the moment completely.

PAYING FOR POSTS

Facebook and Twitter both offer social media managers the chance to promote a post by purchasing strategic message placement with key audiences. While the monetization of social media sites is often a subject of criticism, this system does offer schools and districts the chance to pay a small sum of money (sometimes as little as five dollars) to push a message out to strategically targeted audiences. If you are trying to build your base of fans or followers, or if you have high-quality content or important events, it is worth considering a promoted post.

The important thing to remember about promoted posts or tweets is this: High-quality content is the king of social media. What this means is that the very best, most engaging content will surpass the least engaging content, regardless of payment. The best bet for education leaders—especially those on a limited budget—is to focus less on sponsored posts and much more on creating high-quality, shareable content that engages audience members.

MEASURING YOUR WORK

Social media is a commitment of both time and effort—resources that are limited and must be spent wisely. Learning about your audience on social media allows you to become as strategic and effective as possible with the time and effort you spend. Facebook makes this especially easy by offering scores of data about your posts and fans through Facebook Insights, a feature that is available for free at the fingertips of the page administrator. When it comes time to develop content and messages, it's critical to know the demographics of your audience. For example, administrators on the Eudora Schools Facebook page know from the Insights feature that the page's fans:

- Mostly live within fifty or so miles of the school district
- Are twice as likely to be female than male
- Are typically between the ages of twenty-five and forty-four

To increase the chances of reaching fans of the Eudora district page in the midst of all the social media noise, time is spent monitoring the types of content that are most likely to engage Eudora Schools fans—and the times of day when those fans are most likely to be on Facebook.

Eudora leaders also have been able to use the data from Insights to identify posts that, on the surface, look to be quite average, but that perhaps have more going on behind the scenes. For example, one year on

National Suicide Prevention Day, a post with a link to an external resource was designed to empower the average person to make a difference if they know someone who is considering suicide.

Fan engagement on the Eudora Schools Facebook page tends to be
highest in the late afternoon and early evening hours, but this post was
much different than the content most typically shared on the page because it didn't feature any information about Eudora students or schools.
Rather, this subject reflected a real growth in the number of school-based
support systems the district has provided for the mental health and
healthy development of students and families over the past several years.

For an hour or two after the post went up, engagement appeared to be
minimal. Yet reviewing the post's Insights the next day, it became clear
that it had an incredible level of "reach" — the message had been shown
to more than 1,800 people, making it one of the district's most successful
social media posts at that time. With only fifteen likes and no comments,
it seemed like a dud, but Insights showed that twenty shares — and from
there, many more likes and comments — had turned an average-appear-
ing post into something that really penetrated and made a difference.

This experience also illustrates the varying value of the different types
of engagement in a Facebook post. Here's a clear look at engagement, in
terms of overall reach: Shares > Comments > Likes > Clicks. Shares on
Facebook are, without question, the gold standard of engagement (retweets claim this top engagement spot on Twitter). This engagement will
push your content to an entirely new group of users and followers, and
it's where the reach of Eudora's suicide prevention post really expanded.
Comments and likes are valuable for the interaction of your page, but
they tend not to spread your message to a wider audience in the same
way that shares do. And simple clicks mean that your fans are taking an
interest in your post, but that lower level of engagement fails to widen
the circle of overall reach.

A final consideration for measuring the effectiveness of social media
posts includes tools to track how many people actually click a link that is
provided. For example, bitly.com and other similar sites convert a link
you might have into a unique URL that's short enough to work well in
social networks. When this new web address is clicked, the service will
track the number of clicks that link gets over time and record these statistics using a free online account.

This type of tool helped measure that a post on the district's severe
weather procedures was not as low engagement as it appeared. In fact,
the hundreds of clicks from that post directly to the page on the district
website made it clear that Facebook continues to be a highly effective tool
for driving traffic to specific web-based content. A shortened, trackable
URL also can be extremely useful for Twitter, which limits users to 280
characters per tweet.

LEADERS ON SOCIAL MEDIA

Social media has become a personal communication tool of growing popularity among education leaders. "During our leadership trainings, we've witnessed the use of social media evolve from a source of distraction to a source of positive information," said Mark Dodge, a director at Greenbush–Southeast Kansas Education Service Center. "We encourage districts and school leaders to allow social media to give parents, students, and community members relevant discussions to engage them in real time. In doing so, districts and schools are placing an emphasis on promoting the successes, opportunities, and experiences provided to students. The end result is an overwhelming amount of support and gratitude for districts, schools, staff, and students."

Unlike a district account, which shares a wide range of content from an organizational perspective, a principal, director, or superintendent can use social media—Twitter in particular—to show his or her human interests and emotional investment in the school system. "It's been really cool watching social media become an acceptable and widely used medium for communication by leaders at all levels," Dodge said.

Consider these steps to help ensure a leader's success using a personal Twitter account, or other social media tool, for public engagement:

- A leader's individual account should be designed strategically to promise—and deliver—meaningful content. Spend at least thirty minutes outlining the primary audience, or top two to three audiences you intend to reach with the account, and identifying the type of content that will appeal to, and prompt engagement from, the audience. Think about how much will be original content (tweeting from a classroom that you visit on an average day, or about the high school play) and how much will be shared content (retweeting, for example, the tweets of district teachers, community organizations, and/or leaders in the state). These plans should be written into a short, helpful document to help the leader stay on track, especially when starting out.
- A bio is essentially a preview of the type of content a follower will see. A leader's bio should set the stage for engaging content about the school or district, as identified in the strategic document. Remember that social media has *people* at its heart, and as an education leader you want followers to know that your content will reflect that. Consider the people—kids and adults—who make up your school community, and make sure they're reflected in your content.
- Make good use of the graphic elements in an account. Use a polished photo—ideally somewhere between the standard-issue school photo and a family vacation snapshot. The perfect profile

graphic should look relaxed but professional. A header photo should reflect a personal passion for the school system. These photos are less about branding and more about communicating the values and personality of the leader.

- Decide who you will follow through, and stick to it. Most leaders will follow district teachers and colleagues—that is, after all, a great source of content to share—but may or may not decide to follow students, parents, or community members in general. Every community is different, and regardless of what makes sense in your district, it's best practice to plan ahead and follow through consistently.
- Engage. When followers mention or connect with you on social media, they deserve to know you are listening. Don't miss this chance to reply, or simply "like" their tweet or post. After all, if someone had you on the phone or were standing in your office, you would acknowledge and respond to them. When you are approached on social media with criticism or uncomfortable questions, refer to the strategies in chapter 10 to de-escalate the issue and focus on shared solutions, rather than a debate. Remember, two-way communication can be difficult at times, but the opportunity to build trust is well worth the effort.
- Be consistent. If you tweet one snow day announcement, you'll need to be ready to tweet them all. Try to spread your content out over the hours of the day and days of the week; if a dozen tweets come at one time in the day—say, 5 p.m. when the office is quieting down—it is far less likely that your followers will see your content and engage. An education leader is literally surrounded by great content, every day. Once you adjust to thinking about your audience and the content you want to give them, it will become second nature to pause for sixty seconds and share these posts and stories at all times of the day.

BE STRATEGIC ABOUT YOUR USE

With all the tools available, and all the great features offered in each tool, being strategic is the only real way to avoid being overwhelmed and overextended. Social media may be free and easy to use, but done right, a social media account is a long-term, 24/7 commitment.

In the chronically underfunded world of education, a free tool can be quite tempting. But it's always best to do fewer things really well than to do more things not so well. As your social media confidence grows, you are bound to see new avenues to explore with new accounts. Always begin by choosing one social media account to do well, and then ask yourself these questions before you decide to set up another:

- Will adding a new social media account help me reach a new audience?
- Will the new account help me engage with my existing audience differently, or will it be a duplication of content or effort?
- Am I willing to create original content for each social media account, taking into account the different expectations of Twitter users and Facebook users, for example?
- Can an account be added without sacrificing my ability to monitor and engage in two-way communication (at all hours of the day, through every day of the week) in each social media community?

On the district communications level in Eudora, these questions are considered repeatedly, and each time, the decision has been made to stay with one successful social media account—the district Facebook page. It's true that this page mostly reaches nonstudents, and it's clear that many more of the Eudora Middle School and Eudora High School students are on Instagram and Twitter. However, district leaders also are aware of the very real commitments involved with adding another type of account and managing it equally well. Consequently, a conscious decision was made to manage the district Facebook page very well, and that decision looks to remain both strategic and satisfying for the foreseeable future.

The system-wide embrace of social media has also brought the district to a point where principals and teachers are reaching many more audiences on Twitter, Instagram, and YouTube. For now, these additional school voices on other social media platforms leave room for the district's efforts to remain focused on Facebook. (Not using a tool, however, doesn't mean ignoring it. Review chapter 1 for a reminder about why it's so important—and quite simple—to reserve your identity on the social media platforms you aren't currently using.)

As mentioned in the third question, strategic use of a social media account means creating content that is customized to the platform being used. While it is technically possible to link together different platforms, having Twitter posts automatically populate a Facebook feed, or pushing Facebook updates to the Twitter timeline, should be avoided. Each social media platform creates a community that has unique expectations and content-sharing roles, and these roles are not intended to be interchangeable.

For example, tweets are typically very short with fewer graphics, making them look dull and out of place on a Facebook feed. And Twitter users often must leave Twitter to view an entire message cross-posted from Facebook. Since tweets only contain 240 or fewer characters, Facebook posts that are pushed to Twitter automatically cut off and link back to the original post. Asking a follower to leave one social media platform to continue reading a message on another is the social media version of regularly calling someone on the phone and asking the other person to hang up and call you back on another number. It's a move that lacks both convenience and good manners.

While the ability to link Facebook and Twitter together to save time and reach a bigger audience can be tempting, it is, quite simply, fool's gold. The only way to truly manage a social media presence in the digital world—and maintain and build your school system's online reputation—is by being realistic about your capabilities, and by investing the time and creating the content to do it right.

FACEBOOK BASICS

It's been a long time since Facebook was the only popular social media site, but it can still be a great choice for schools and districts. In fact, the experience in Eudora shows that Facebook can be an extremely popular online community for one of the most important stakeholder groups: parents of current students. For that reason, most Eudora teachers have embraced it for work first, before Twitter, Instagram, YouTube, or others. Here are a few details that are critical to the effective use of Facebook for schools and classrooms:

- According to Facebook's terms of service, a person is allowed only one personal profile—no more. Teachers and administrators should not set up a separate profile for work, but instead use a page or group. Your fans should "like" your Facebook page or ask to be invited to your Facebook group—*not* send a friend request. Friend requests indicate that a personal profile is being used, rather than a page or group.
- Remember that users must be thirteen years old to open a Facebook account. Students and some parents may not observe this rule, but it's critical that education leaders respect it and plan social networking activities accordingly.
- Facebook pages and groups must be tied back to the manager's personal profile page. (Don't worry, this won't affect who can see your own private or personal information, and in the case of a Facebook page, nobody will ever see whose profile is tied to the account.)
- Facebook pages provide a way to share text updates, photos, videos, and events. A page can be viewed by anyone on the web, with or without a Facebook account; a Facebook user must be logged in, however, to have the ability to like or comment on the page.
- Facebook groups offer a range of privacy settings, often making them better suited to share more intimate information, including student's first and last names, lists of classroom volunteers, or class schedules and routines. Groups also allow for the sharing of docu-

ments, such as fliers, menus, and assignments. "Secret" groups are the most private and can also be a great tool for professional networking among colleagues in a school.

In the end, online communities are not so different from IRL communities—there are norms, expectations, and distinct languages. But these currencies should never be a barrier to getting started. A social media manager need only watch and listen—basic empathy skills that educators use every day—to learn how to communicate best in any given social media community.

KEY IDEAS TO REMEMBER

- Social media posts should be written using friendly, familiar language—the same vocabulary and sentence structure that you would use speaking to a friend or family member.
- Great content highlights the people and places that your followers love, the information they want, and calm leadership during difficult times.
- Leaders who personally and strategically use social media can build trust and support for their district and schools. Planning your use before beginning will increase the value and success of your chosen social media; give special thought to your target audience(s) and the content you wish to deliver to each.
- A hashtag is a powerful tool on Twitter and other networks for finding topics of interest and participating in relevant, dynamic conversations about those topics with people around the globe.
- Live video offers perhaps the most engaging content on social media, allowing parents and community members a front-row seat to the engagement, learning, and love that is modeled in your school each day. Spend time to understand the special considerations of live video, in order to reap the greatest reward.
- The key to successful social networking relies on your message standing out in the fast-moving information flow of the digital world. Paying for post promotion can be useful in certain situations, but *the single most effective way of getting a message through is creating great social content*—especially posts that use photos, videos, and links to useful resources to tell stories or meet the needs of fans and followers.
- Data should drive an education leader's decisions about content and timing, particularly on Facebook. Facebook page managers should regularly review the page's Facebook Insights to understand the demographics of those who make up the digital community, and then refine content and posting strategies.

- When it comes to social media strategy, more is not better. Effectively managing a presence on multiple accounts requires intentional content creation, monitoring, and interacting. The addition of a new active account must always reflect a strategic advantage.
- Every social networking site has its own set of user guidelines and terms of service. It's the responsibility of anyone managing a social media account to make sure these are understood and followed, without exception.

EIGHT
Teaching and Learning

For generations, middle and high school students have learned letter writing as a critical skill for college, career, and life. From the address and salutation to the closing, students learn and practice this all-important communications product. Of course, the earliest keyboarding skills are now learned when toddlers first start tapping and swiping the touch screen on a tablet or smartphone. But despite the obvious changes in technologies, basic letter-writing skills—extended to also include email correspondence—are as essential as ever to the success of college students and professionals across a wide range of fields.

However, adequately preparing students for college and careers, and equipping them with the academic, social, and emotional tools for work and life, requires school systems and teachers to also address students' communication skills on social networks. After all, it's rare that a printed letter or email message would cause someone to be passed over for an interview, much less lose a job. A social media post, by contrast, can have this effect swiftly, and often without warning.

Embedding social media in the classroom helps equip students, beginning even before middle school, with the skills and judgment to help them become effective communicators in the spaces where it can count most. And now with well-designed policy, procedures, and professional development in place, you've opened the doors wide to enormous opportunities for teaching and learning citizenship skills—and so much more—in the digital world.

REAL-WORLD RELEVANCE

Alabama principal Angie Bush, who previously taught high school French, used Twitter in her classroom regularly to practice simple written conversation skills, but those activities also opened up the door to other important conversations. "I used Twitter with my French students because it was free, quick, and everyone had access. I loved it when people from outside my class would interact with us. If the conversation was inappropriate, we would talk about how to report the user to Twitter and follow those steps. This helped my students know what to do—how to report it—if something similar came up outside of the classroom."

As more teachers in a district become active on Twitter, it presents a natural opportunity for leaders to encourage sharing and collaboration—and harness the power of teacher-created content to build a broader district culture. As Twitter adoption increased in Deerfield Public School District 109 in Illinois, leaders chose a hashtag to help teachers and administrators share with and invest in one another, regardless of where their classroom or office is located.

"Our district hashtag, #engage109, has become a window into, as well as a reflection of, our culture," said Cathy Kedjidjian, coordinator of communications and community relations. "Staff use it to share ideas and resources with each other, to connect with educators and experts worldwide, and to give parents, community members, and prospective employees a real-time view into the classroom and the values that define our district."

One of the favorite benefits reported by teachers using social media is the relevance that these networks provide—a worldwide stage where they can share their reflections, ideas, images, and work. Kyle Stadalman, a Eudora Elementary School fifth-grade teacher and social media champion, made it simple and clear: "When I tell students I will be posting their work to Facebook or uploading a video to YouTube, the quality of work and dedication to the task rises significantly. It suddenly becomes serious because students are thinking, 'My teacher and classmates aren't the only ones who will see my work.'"

Stadalman uses his classroom Facebook page strategically, posting photos and occasional live videos of classroom activities. He also uses it as a learning lab for one specific language arts skill that he said students tend to struggle with—summarization. "Summarizing our school day each afternoon is a way to have our class reflect on what we've done, and it creates a natural opportunity for us to practice organizing those reflections into a summary. I have students post these summaries on Facebook for two reasons—first, it makes the work feel important to the student who gets to stand at my laptop and carefully type while the class follows along on our Promethean board. But also, it gives my students' parents a great snapshot of what we've been doing all day."

Stadalman said he also has found that social media can be particularly effective when he has important announcements or reminders for parents. "If I need to send out a reminder about an event, I will usually have a student write it on a piece of paper and then take a picture of the student holding the note. I know it will get viewed by more people if it's a picture."

Kristin Merrill, intermediate teacher in Collier County Public Schools in Florida, credits her experience on Twitter for much of her recent growth as an educator, especially when she found herself as a newcomer in a tightly knit school setting. "Social media was my escape from the awkwardness of not fitting in at first," Merrill said. "It allowed me to share who I was and get my name and teaching style out to the parents and staff at this new school. It was a way for me to communicate without having to speak. It was a way for me to share my best practices without waiting to be asked."

But she is convinced that the benefits have extended far beyond her first few months in a new classroom. "It has led to more technology and better teaching practices not only at our school," she said, "but at our district level. It has fostered collaboration and creativity well outside my four classroom walls. It has also led to cross-country friendships and collaboration with numerous educational apps. It has transformed me from a remedial educator to a reflective innovator."

His teenage students may be older and wiser than the average fourth or fifth grader, but Eudora High School video instructor Nate Robinson finds that the real-time, real-world stage provided on social networks is just as important to his students when it comes time to complete their class projects, which range from sports team highlight videos and broadcasts to creative skits and informational or persuasive video messages. "Putting videos on YouTube and sharing out through Twitter and Facebook does huge things for the content that my students create. Before we used YouTube, the only people who would see our videos were the other students in my class. Now we can post a video and tweet or link to it, and hundreds of people get to see what we make. It puts the pressure on to make better videos, as well, when you know how many people are watching."

Not surprisingly, the high school video students are often quick to jump on whatever video trend is going around, making social networks the perfect fit. And whether it's a local version of a Justin Timberlake video or a new take on a Jimmy Fallon skit, Robinson has found that these generate hundreds, if not thousands, of views over a very short time. "I strive to get a lot of hits on our videos—not just to collect a view count, but to reach further out into the community so people can see the students and activities that go on at Eudora High School. We've been doing these videos for some time now, but if you look back at our activity since our district embraced social media, you'll see a difference. There is a huge increase when we started posting our videos on Facebook, and once we had several hundred followers there, our view count went up fast. It's an amazing thing to be able to produce content that people like, and to provide that content in a place and on a device where they want to view it."

Even without using an external social network, blogging tools can achieve the real-world relevance that enriches student learning. For example, Stadalman uses a Wordpress blog as an online discussion board for his fifth-grade classroom. "This gives each student an equal voice — and when you're online, no one gets interrupted or runs out of time telling a story. The ability to reply to others helps create a sense of community and togetherness among the students. I moderate the discussion board to keep it on topic and appropriate, but I love that we can spend a half hour with twenty-five students all sharing stories and replying to others, in a room that is dead silent."

HASHTAGS TO EXTEND THE CLASSROOM

As explained in chapter 7, hashtags are short phrases preceded by the pound sign (#) that group together related content and locate existing discussions on virtually any topic. For this reason, hashtags can become powerful tools in the hands of a classroom teacher.

A science teacher and social media champion at Eudora High School, Eric Magette has found hashtags to be a key to engaging his students on social media, both in and out of class. He chose a hashtag for all of his science classes—#RoomE102, which refers to the science lab room—for him and his students to use. "I made up a hashtag for all of my science classes, and I use it any time that I tweet about what's going on in our classroom," he said. "Those tweets might include photos of a dissection lab, reflections on the content, or sometimes a cartoon or funny story. On the days when we are engaged in something really visual, I also encourage my students to upload their photos from class to Twitter or Instagram and use the hashtag. I'm able to follow all of those tweets by just monitoring our hashtag, and when I see a student tweet a photo of something from class, I'm quick to retweet it or engage with the students in other ways."

An avid Twitter user, he also follows a handful of popular hashtags, including #scied. It was in that Twitter discussion one day that he came across a high school science teacher halfway across the country who was planning to have his students "live tweet" (post tweets during an event, program, or broadcast) an upcoming documentary on public television.

Adopting the idea himself—as well as the hashtag that the other teacher had coined—Magette made an announcement to *his* students that they could get a few points of extra credit if they watched the program that evening and tweeted about it. "It was so powerful to see my students, in our small town, at home on their own time, tweeting about a show that ties directly to our curriculum," he said, reflecting on the experience.

"And then, to know that my students were connecting and sharing ideas with science students on the East Coast—that's something that I would never have even dreamed of just a few years prior. It just couldn't happen without social media." He later used the online tool Storify to publish all the related tweets in one place, sharing the final results with his students and with the other science teacher who first hatched the project.

Though native to Twitter, hashtags have become an integral part of the way other social networking sites work, as well, including Instagram. This is one more tool that can be used to extend learning beyond the classroom by tagging photos about similar topics. Take, for example, a social studies unit on an important period in your state's history. A simple assignment could be for students to take and share a photo of a landmark, or evidence of an important local historic experience, such as the Dust Bowl. A teacher need only monitor the hashtag within Instagram to see the completed student work. The teacher can make constructive comments on the photos to provide more information or context about the photo or lesson. Science and math concepts are found in a wide range of daily activities, and extending these concepts into the real world creates a level of immediacy and a relevancy difficult to replicate in a classroom.

DIGITAL CITIZENSHIP

Whether posting a daily summary on Facebook, contributing content to an Instagram discussion, preparing a video for YouTube, or live-tweeting a relevant television program, using social media in the classroom offers students opportunities to learn how to be productive citizens in the digital world while also learning and practicing the timeless language arts skills of grammar, punctuation, and spelling that are essential for all types of communication.

But they also are learning how to think like digital citizens, with ongoing reminders that their posts on social networks are both public and permanent. They are learning about social and emotional skills that matter just as much online as they do in real life—skills and habits such as respect, honesty, resilience, and kindness. It can be understandably daunting for a teacher to start using social media to teach these skills, especially if the teacher is not entirely comfortable with the tools to begin with.

"As educators, we're always behind the curve when it comes to technology," said Curtis Chandler, a former Kansas middle school English teacher who now works as an educational consultant. "By the time we get comfortable with Facebook, or Twitter, or Instagram, our students have moved on to the next thing. Instead of making that the problem, we need to look for ways to involve students more. They're the ones tinkering in social media—they'll find the next thing before we do. If we listen to them and ask them how these tools can be used for learning, I think we'll hear some really good ideas."

While embedding social media in student learning activities gives students great opportunities to understand how these relevant tools can be used productively, schools must take responsibility for building a curriculum that explicitly addresses digital citizenship. Whether this topic falls to librarians/media specialists, technology teachers, or even core subject teachers, it is now a critical component of preparing students for success in school and after graduation.

PARENTS AS EMPOWERED PARTNERS

Teachers in Eudora also have found that using social media in the classroom brings an added element of parent engagement and participation. "I was a little reluctant about using social media in my classroom at first," said Eudora fifth-grade teacher and social media champion Niki Rheuport. "I probably never would have used social media for my class without the encouragement of my district, but it's become a great part of my classroom community. And I can say now, after several years of using it, that parent communication has never been easier and better all the way around."

Rheuport's first-grade colleague, teaching veteran Becky Topil, finds that most of her students' families are hungry for the kind of interaction that a closed Facebook group provides. In addition to the quick updates and photos from the school day, Topil takes full advantage of the events feature, reminding her families about picture day, early release schedules, music programs, and other special activities. She takes the weekly lunch menu and posts a "translated" version with picture illustrations for her prereading students, and takes opportunities to share live videos to help classroom parents enjoy a look at daily activities. She even uses the group to ask for help when she needs another box of Kleenex or bottle of hand sanitizer, and she has found that parents are always quick to respond.

But she realized just how important the tool was becoming—even in a first-grade environment—when one day in the early fall, a student came and told her that his parents wanted to see photographs of what their routine looked like each day.

> It almost shocked me to have a first grader tell me that we should post photos of our routines on Facebook because his mom and dad wanted to know more about his day. That just goes to show that social media is

part of the conversation at home! As we discussed it in our classroom, my students—just six and seven years old at the time—decided that we should take photos of all the parts of our day. I used my phone to take pictures of our class reciting the morning pledge, lining up for specials, getting out our supplies, and doing all of the little things that we do each day. Once those were posted, our parents just loved it because they could now visualize exactly the things that their children were talking about in the evening, and they could ask questions and have more conversations about the day. It has been great.

A lesson learned in Eudora over the course of the district's social media embrace is just how much parents—and virtually all adults—still have to learn. While social media can be second nature to students, parents often feel at least a little lost when it comes to keeping their child safe and healthy online. And in the always-changing world of social networking, it's easy for a parent to feel like he or she barely knows enough to keep up, much less to provide appropriate guidelines, expectations, and consequences for tweens and teens.

It's not uncommon for school principals to be made aware of bullying behavior on the latest—and often most opaque—social media site. This is exactly what happened in late 2013 when now-retired Eudora Middle School principal Denise Kendall began receiving parent calls about a new social networking site that was all but unknown to the administrators in our district before that point. "It was such a surprise," Kendall said, "mostly because nobody here had even heard of the site—except for the kids. And the kids all said that it was a problem."

It was a problem because the site was set up so that people could leave anonymous comments about users with little monitoring or control. A quick Google search about the site itself turned up horror stories of young people actually dying by suicide after allegedly being bullied on this particular site. "I knew we needed to help our parents," Kendall reflected. "I knew that they needed to know more about the site, but also about what to do to help their children."

It was at this point that a guide for parents was developed—posted on the district website and shared regularly in school newsletters and with district and school Facebook followers—to empower them with valuable information about social networks, including age restrictions and guidelines, as well as tips about privacy settings. This guide also includes links to resources that can help prevent and report bullying behavior, as well as encouragement for parents to take an active role in their child's life online. Kendall said,

> When we had the incident with the new site, it was a huge reminder that our parents want to be partners in this. They want to help their children have a positive experience online, but so often they don't know where to start because their children know more about these sites than they do. We've found that giving parents basic information

about social networks is a good place to start. And from there, we remind them that, really, this is just like any other kind of parenting because it's about keeping the conversation open between parents and kids. If you can ask your son or daughter who they will be hanging out with on a Friday night, you should also ask about the experiences they're having on social media. Those conversations may not be easy, but they are the best way to make sure kids are supported and guided as they're growing up in a digital world.

Social media's power is great in the realm of teaching and learning, especially when it allows parents and families to become a direct part of that process. But as engaging as social media can be in the classroom, educators cannot be content simply to encourage the use of social media as a teaching tool. They must also accept the responsibility to teach and model positive, constructive use of social media to students and parents alike.

KEY IDEAS TO REMEMBER

- Learning to effectively communicate on social media is an essential twenty-first-century skill that students need to be successful in life after high school.
- Using social media tools for student learning activities brings an engaging, real-world relevance for students of all ages.
- Hashtags offer teachers and administrators a free, familiar tool to extend the student learning experience outside of the classroom, and often even outside of the school day.
- In addition to more traditional academic content, a teacher's use of social media in any classroom becomes a natural way to teach students critical digital citizenship skills.
- Social media is a great channel to reach parents of students, giving any parent an accessible, engaging role in the classroom community. It's also an opportunity to support and empower parents as they learn about the sites their children are using and talking about.

NINE

Communicating with Families and Other Stakeholders

Even the most thriving school districts stand to gain from the strategic use of social media. "We've got a great district," said elementary principal John Cannon in the small rural community of Lyons, Kansas. "But one of the things that was stressed to us by our patrons and our board was that we needed more outreach between our schools and the community at large. Even though we have a terrific district, we needed to communicate that and make sure we were the ones telling our story. Social media tools are what we can use to add that next layer of communications."

Social media is built for communication, and this set of outreach-minded tools available through various platforms offers enormous benefits to schools and school districts. Website updates, backpack fliers, email messages, SMS text, and phone calls still have an important place in the way that schools and districts communicate with families and other stakeholder groups. The use of social media, though, brings a dynamic new dimension to a school system's outreach efforts. And although social media tools may be newer, and they may look and feel different than the newsletters and town hall meetings education leaders are most accustomed to, the fundamentals of communication are exactly the same:

- Know your audience. Who are you trying to reach with your message? Whether parents, employees, patrons, students, or other stakeholder groups, there are specific characteristics to keep in mind. Each group will be motivated by different things, they will be open to messages at different times of the day, and they likely will go to different places to find those messages. Knowing your audience and their habits is the single most important step in communicating, and social media is no exception.

- Identify your goals. Messages are only effective when they support a bigger goal. What do you want your audience to know, and, more importantly, why do you want them to know it? Do you want them to take action on something—update their schedule, volunteer in the library, fill out a form, or contact their legislator? Perhaps the message is supportive of a bigger school- or district-level value or goal, such as increasing high academic standards, building positive community relations, or bringing greater transparency to district operations. Articulating the goal of your message typically requires only a few moments, but the time spent ensures that you are making a constructive contribution to your audience's information pipeline.
- Timing is everything. Communicating a message involves decisions about how soon the information needs to go out (instantly, within a few hours, within a few days, or at a specific point in the future). With your audience clearly identified, you can also make decisions about *when* your message should go out. Just as there are days of the week and times of day when employees are most likely to open an email (probably *not* 6:30 p.m. on a Friday), there are days and times when employees—or any other stakeholders—are more likely to notice a message on social media. Learn how to pinpoint these times using your Facebook Insights, a simple online survey, or the abundant data widely available about social media user behavior.
- Find the right channel. If your target audience is parents, find out where your parents are. The Eudora Schools Facebook page is made up of a large number of parents and employees, but Eudora students are likely to be found on other social media channels. Choosing the right channel will help ensure that your message reaches the right audience, at the right time. And keep in mind that it's still best to share certain messages through an email, newsletter, or meeting. Social media doesn't replace other tools; it simply puts another set of options in your communications toolbox.

TUNE INTO STATION WII-FM

At the end of the day, working through the questions of audience, timing, and channel will only help your message reach your audience if you tune into Station WII-FM—*What's In It For Me?*—because the fact is, it doesn't matter what an education leader wants to say, or what he or she wants people to know. It doesn't even matter what he or she *needs* them to know.

On any given day, audiences are being bombarded with messages and information from all sides. For a message to somehow penetrate the information overload, it must resonate with an audience member in a way that fills a personal need. Think of WII-FM as that station that comes in the strongest and clearest in the car and, consequently, is the one you are most likely to have on. It's the place to hear the need-to-know information that makes a person's day run smoothly. As education leaders and communicators, only the messages that hit that same frequency stand a real chance of engaging our audience's attention or prompting action.

When preparing a message to share—through social media or any communications tool—there are two questions to consider. First, is this message naturally important to the audience? In the case of parents in a school district, naturally important messages might include snow days, crisis updates, and specific health information that directly and immediately affects their student. The fact that you have information that is *genuinely* important does not mean that it is *naturally* important to the people you are trying to reach.

Next (and especially if the answer to the first question is *no*), what priorities or values do you share with your audience? For example, school districts need students to be in school, so tardiness and absenteeism are often priorities, and attendance reminders to parents are a natural solution. But an administrative need for kids to be in school isn't likely to sincerely motivate a parent in the same way that it motivates school personnel. Instead, frame your attendance message to parents around what matters to parents—how will having a child in school make mom's or dad's life easier?

Keep in mind that this frame must be something that an audience member would agree makes his or her life better or easier. If you aren't sure, spend a few minutes talking to sample members of your audience about the issue to understand what truly motivates them.

WHAT WORKS—AND WINS

Having discussed the ways that social media is similar to more traditional communications tools, there are important—and powerful—characteristics that truly set it apart. As reviewed in chapter 1, social networking sites provide a level of two-way communication and social sharing that simply does not exist anywhere else. Even the best newsletter, or the most crowded meeting, will never have the staying and sharing power of a message communicated through social media.

When it comes down to harnessing that power at its peak, great content is king. Including photos, videos, and links to resources are all ways to increase engagement for the messages you share on social media. Even text-only information that is highly engaging to your audience—and shareable to a wider audience—will be both powerful and effective.

So, what engages people in social media content? Education leaders in Eudora have found that parents are highly interested in what's happening in schools and activities, day in and day out. Certainly, the latest piece of good news is popular, but parents and other followers also engage regularly with simple updates and positive posts.

One example is a Twitter account managed by Cara Kimberlin, activities director and assistant principal at Eudora High School. Kimberlin uses the account to provide information about activities and schedules, scoring updates from games and tournaments, and general information about her school and high school activities in the region. "For years, people in town were telling me they wanted scores and updates from games," Kimberlin said. "It got to a point where people were texting me during big games, or posting on the district Facebook page on a Friday night, asking for game updates. We can't always respond to those, and we didn't want our Facebook page to get overrun with sports updates, but Twitter seemed like the perfect way to streamline those updates so that people could get them on their own, and all in one place."

When a big game approaches, the district Facebook page includes a post announcing that scoring updates will be available through the Twitter account, which is also threaded through an application to a tab on the district's Facebook page. Fans are able to watch scoring updates on Twitter, or right on Facebook if they prefer. In addition to game updates, Kimberlin also uses the account to retweet content that students and teachers have already shared. "I enjoy retweeting photos of great learning in our classrooms, or comments from players getting geared up for a big game because it reminds our followers that there are great things happening all over our school, and that the players we put on the field are proud to be representing us."

Including the additional content helps Kimberlin make the requisite list of scores and schedule changes more personal and engaging by painting a bigger picture of the dynamics of high school life—something that has the power to capture the imagination of nearly anyone who has attended high school before. And when a big game is on the line, sharing the tweets from players and students before and after the game—win or lose—also tells the bigger story of the high school experience.

"People are captivated by stories," said Ben Smith, the consultant who advised Eudora Schools leaders during the district's embrace of social media. "If you can make someone smile, laugh, or cry, you have engaging content. It isn't complicated—people will engage with the things that they value, and schools are a great example of the things that people have an emotional attachment to. They're proud; they're excited about what's happening in their child's school. If you just tell those stories, you will be successful."

Two Eudora Middle School students were featured in a regional newspaper after traveling to nearby Lawrence for a special event. One of these students, whose disabilities require him to use a wheelchair, had participated in a Special Olympics clinic with the women's basketball team at the University of Kansas. A classmate and friend accompanied him that day in KU's famed Allen Fieldhouse to help him get around and enjoy the clinic. When a photo that included both of these students was featured on the newspaper's photo gallery, it made perfect sense to share it with the district's Facebook followers.

Following a quick phone conversation with the participant's mother to make sure the family would be comfortable with it, the post immediately caught fire with the district's Facebook supporters. This photo, with very little added explanation, moved the parents, students, employees, and community members on the page. It inspired fans to feel proud of the great students in the schools and community, and it likely prompted smiles and — occasionally — goose bumps or watery eyes.

As a result, leaders were able to instantly share a feel-good story in a way that prompted impressive engagement through clicks, likes, comments, and shares. The Facebook Insights on that post illustrate that great content, even when it's simple and shared from somewhere else, trumps everything else on social media when there is an emotional connection to the audience.

BUILD A PLATFORM FOR COMMUNICATION

After considering the uses of social networks for teaching and learning, it's important to examine how these tools can be used to communicate the school and district messages that have been developed according to the guidelines already laid out in this chapter. "The most important thing is to focus on building a community," Smith said, "not just building a page. If you build a community where people interact and share information and resources, you have created a great deal of value. And those are the places where social media users will actually go and visit, rather than just waiting for the information to come to them. People go to resources because they value them."

Building that community is exciting, but it can also trigger some of the fears that were covered in chapter 2. *What if someone posts something inappropriate or nasty — something that could potentially hurt our district, students, or employees?* Undoubtedly, two-way communication can be uncomfortable at times. By now, though, you understand that the risks can be mitigated by carefully thinking through the policies, procedures, and professional development strategies laid out in previous chapters. And it's worth noting again that, done properly, the benefits that accompany a social media community far outweigh the risks and trouble.

Ray Winkler, principal of Sloan Creek Intermediate in Fairview, Texas, uses Twitter and Facebook extensively to communicate with employees, students, and parents. He has learned to manage those tools in a positive way by making sure that people believe they have personal, direct access to him. He explained:

> You don't want social media to be the only way to communicate. I give out my cell phone number at every school assembly and put it on each whiteboard when we have a substitute on campus, for the guest teacher and the leaders. It's also in the weekly video email I send to kids and parents. There must be an avenue to open up communication to people who have a question or problem, and it should be easier to text the principal than it is to tweet it or put it on Facebook.
>
> This keeps so many of the negative questions and comments off of social media because we've established that it's a positive place where we celebrate the great things happening at school, not a place where we go to air dirty laundry or make a complaint. Even if you don't want to give out your cell phone number, you can get a Google number or find another way to give people simple, immediate access. Doing that will go a long way toward keeping your social media sites positive.

The communications potential of both Facebook and Twitter can extend even beyond those students, parents, employees, or fans who use those sites. As mentioned in chapter 7, a Facebook page is actually a website accessible to anyone, even without logging in. Users must be logged in to interact with posts, but even without, users can see all the content and follow links to the photos, videos, or other resources that have been posted. With this in mind, it makes great sense to include the link to your Facebook page in virtually any electronic or printed communication sent to parents and patrons, because even someone without a Facebook account can still view and enjoy the content provided there.

Likewise, people can follow Twitter users and hashtags without logging in or even creating an account. As long as a Twitter user's tweets are made available publicly, they can be read by anyone entering a specific user or hashtag in any internet search engine, such as Google. Twitter also provides a way for people to receive tweets, even without using the site. The 40404 feature allows anyone to subscribe to specific tweets via SMS text messaging. By texting "Follow (username)" to the number 40404, anyone with a cell phone can receive every one of that user's tweets as a text message.

The 40404 function has great potential for Twitter accounts that provide regular updates about attendance days, schedule changes, sports scores, or crisis information. Those are the WII-FM topics that will motivate people to subscribe—and once they are subscribed and receiving the information they want, they also will be viewing and reading the good news and other announcements that are the most important to *you*.

The potential power of hashtags is never as evident as during a crisis or emergency. Such events typically result in a flood of tweets, and a hashtag often emerges early to help aggregate the fast-paced conversation into one feed. In Southlake, Texas, leaders at Carroll Independent School District—whose mascot is the dragons—saw the potential and created a go-to hashtag for all safety-related messages. "Operation #SAFEdragon began in 2013 shortly after the shootings at Sandy Hook Elementary School when our school resource officer program was expanded to include all campuses," said Julie Thannum, assistant superintendent for board and community relations. "We lacked cohesive messaging that was targeted for safety topics. Operation #SAFEdragon (Safety Awareness For Every Dragon) is a multifaceted response plan that affects all facilities and departments. The program includes a number of initiatives aimed at fortifying buildings, ensuring regular training, communication, and increasing staff and public awareness."

But the hashtag quickly went to work on the district's social media channels, from bad weather days and facility lockdowns, to transportation, road hazards, or water main breaks. Thannum said, "Our parents, students, and staff watch for #SAFEdragon posts on Twitter, Facebook, and even through our Mobile Dragon mobile app. With more than 12,200 Twitter followers and nearly 6,000 followers on Facebook, we can get instant safety messaging out to a large internal and external audience."

And, as with so many things on social media, a formal effort was adopted by a larger, informal audience and has reached a new level of influence. Thannum explained, "We've had kids tweet pictures back to us of #SAFEdragon written in the snow on their windshields and lawn furniture. Students in neighboring districts have coined the term with their mascot during bad weather days, as they communicate through their own district or personal social media channels. It really is fixed in our culture."

GROW A COMMUNITY

To extend beyond simply constructing a site, and toward building a community, education leaders must think like museum curators and move past a message-by-message approach to content. Loosely defined, the role of a museum curator is to collect and arrange pieces of work that help interpret a certain heritage, culture, history, or movement. For a school system, managing a social media account is grounded in the work of curating content in a way that helps tell the story of your schools and district, including their mission, culture, vision, and goals.

Content that is posted or tweeted should reflect the most important stories you are trying to tell. The most successful social media accounts are clear and focused; people know what they will find, they know the kinds of messages they will see, and they understand the resources that are being made available by a school or district. When audience members know that what you are posting aligns with their interests and values, your fan base—and, more importantly, your fans' engagement—will grow.

It can be daunting for social media managers who are facing the prospect of building a fan base out of virtually nothing. But remember that even the pages or users with hundreds of thousands of likes or follows once had just two or three. Attracting and adding fans and followers is, first and foremost, the result of the content you share. Districts large and small report that one of the best chances for growing the number of followers or fans comes in the hours leading up to a possible "snow day" announcement, as every parent and student hopes to get that news as soon as it's announced.

On more typical days, your focus should be on the tools embedded within social media that can help you grow and expand your audience. Don't be shy about the account you are managing—freely ask your colleagues, friends, and family members to like or follow it. Periodically remind your existing fans to invite their friends to like or follow your account. And when you notice that you are approaching a milestone number—100, 1,500, 10,000, or whatever number feels good to you—take the opportunity to post a simple message, such as "We've almost hit 1,000 fans—invite your friends and show your Cardinal pride!"

But even as you occasionally ask others to recruit new fans and followers, remember that the most important thing you can do as curator is to create content that resonates with your audience. After all, even friends and family will be less than enthusiastic to click "like" or "follow" if the content available doesn't spark their interest or engage their emotions.

LET YOUR FANS POST

One of the fears education leaders must overcome in the social media embrace is allowing fans and followers to post publicly on a Facebook page. "No way—we don't even want to go there," confided a top district-level administrator in a large urban district who helps manage the district's Facebook page and its more than ten thousand fans. On the surface, this attitude is understandable, as there can be uncomfortable moments and issues to address; strategies for handling difficult situations will be covered in chapter 10. But rather than focusing on what could go wrong when you can't control all the content, this is yet another time to focus on the opportunities available.

Think about the iconic moments at school: the first day in a new school year, Halloween and Valentine's Day parties in elementary classrooms, science fairs, field days, homecoming, prom, and graduation. These are the events that already engage parents, students, and families across a school district, and in the world of smartphones, digital photography, and social media, these events are well documented and ready to be shared.

What better opportunity to ask your fans to post or tweet their favorite photos—and include you? Imagine the engagement that is possible when parents and students start posting their favorite photos on your page, tagging your handle in a tweet, or posting with a hashtag that you have created.

Social media played a big role in Eudora when the boys' basketball team won the first state title in school history. The championship game took place several hours away, on the first Saturday of spring break, but watching what students and fans were posting and tweeting made it the perfect opportunity to ask for help. A simple request—*Post or tweet us your favorite shot of Cardinal fans cheering in the arena!*—yielded photo after photo of the crowd, the fans, and the community that had come out to support the team.

The same strategy works well in a school system all year long. Consider the number of competitions, activities, and projects where students are participating, but you are not able to attend or share on social media yourself. Each of these events, no matter how small they may seem in the big picture, offers an opportunity for school and district leaders to connect with stakeholders and increase the reach of their social media presence.

On the Eudora Schools Facebook page, parents and employees have posted outstanding content about everything from FFA, SkillsUSA, and music festivals, to classroom projects and special activities. Allowing fans to post on your page, or otherwise submit content to you through social media, gives you the ability to recognize and celebrate a much greater range of school activities and accomplishments than you could ever cover on your own. When fans post to a Facebook page, however, don't forget that very few people will see it. The role of an account manager in these cases is to make sure great content gets shared, whenever possible, to the main page so all followers and fans can appreciate it.

Encouraging others to contribute content accomplishes two important things. First, it creates great shareable content for the page manager to use on the fly and without a burdensome investment of time. Second—and most importantly—it engages fans and followers as partners, contributors, and storytellers in our message. Remember, neither of these great outcomes is possible if fans and followers are blocked from making contributions to your page.

COMMUNITY GUIDELINES

One of the most important elements of building a positive and engaging social media community is to create, post, and share clear expectations about how fans and followers are expected to behave and interact within the community. These guidelines articulate boundaries of behavior for fans, but they also provide a framework for the education leaders who manage the page to monitor and moderate content and interactions within the social media community.

Here are the community guidelines posted across school-level and district-level Facebook pages in Eudora Schools:

> Welcome to the official Facebook Page for Eudora Schools. This page is intended to provide updated information and discussion on Eudora Schools and to serve as a resource for our parents, students, teachers and staff, and our local community. The page provides an open forum for you to ask questions and share your opinions and experiences. While we are making this an open forum, we ask that you show respect for your fellow users if you comment on our page by ensuring the discussion remains respectful and family friendly, especially since Facebook allows children as young as 13 to join. In addition to keeping it family friendly, we ask that you adhere to the Comment Policy we have set out below. Comments and posts that do not follow these guidelines may be removed.
>
> Comment Policy: Eudora Schools USD 491 encourages interaction from Facebook users but is not responsible for comments or wall postings made by visitors to the page. Additionally, the appearance of external links, as posted by fans of this page or other Facebook users, does not constitute endorsement on behalf of Eudora Schools USD 491.
>
> Please be aware that all content and posts are bound by Facebook's Terms of Use.
>
> You should not provide private or personal information (phone, email, addresses, etc.) regarding yourself or others on this page. Any posts or comments containing personal information of this nature will be deleted.
>
> We reserve the right, but assume no obligation, to remove comments that are racist, sexist, abusive, profane, violent, obscene, spam, contain falsehoods or are wildly off-topic, or that libel, incite, threaten or make ad hominem attacks on students, employees, guests or other individuals. We also do not permit messages selling products or promoting commercial or other ventures.
>
> You participate at your own risk, taking personal responsibility for your comments, your username and any information provided.
>
> We encourage you to share your support for our students and connect with other supporters here on our page, and to visit frequently for news and updates.

(The first and last name and contact information for the primary manager of the Facebook page also is included at the end of the policy.)

Guidelines are just one piece of the equation for creating the best social media community for a school or district; education leaders play an important role in reinforcing these expectations. The work of creating and maintaining a respectful and constructive social media community depends on the content and tone of administrative voice, as well as the consistency by which the guidelines are enforced.

"When we have abusive users on our Facebook page, we don't turn a blind eye," said a communications professional who manages district social media accounts for an affluent school district. "We are clear about our expectations, and we are serious about enforcing them. There are too many good people who are in our community to share, support, learn, and celebrate; I am not going to allow the few exceptions to this ruin the experience for our larger community."

If someone comments or posts content that conflicts with the posted guidelines (see the example earlier in this chapter), the administrator should contact the person privately, if possible. A direct message is a swift way to inform the user that his or her post or comment has been removed, and remind the user that he or she may be blocked if guidelines are not followed in the future.

Most often, a violation of guidelines is the result of a heated debate, or simple lack of awareness that guidelines exist. However, account moderators should stand firm in their enforcement of expectations—your school community deserves nothing less. See chapter 10 for additional guidance on addressing negative or nasty comments within your social media community.

TELL YOUR STORY

Social networks give schools and school districts the chance to tell their story, rather than leaving that job to others. From celebrating good news to apologizing when things go wrong, and everything in between, social media provides a worldwide stage where education leaders can carve out an identity, brand, and story. David Smith, chief of staff for the large urban school district in Kansas City, Kansas, considers it this way:

> I look at our district's Facebook page as prime real estate. As we develop that real estate, aesthetics are very important. We work hard to develop our photography skills because we want to post things that will engage you visually—you're going to see it before you read it—and entice you to click. If it continues to be engaging, users will continue to click through.
>
> If we post a dozen photographs of people smiling at a camera, holding a certificate, we'll lose you. But if the photos are different,

engaging, and interesting, we'll keep you. And, most importantly, we will be establishing our brand for our families, employees, and patrons—something that they can be proud of. When our page is visually interesting enough that people want to engage with it, it imprints a positive image of the district in their mind. That's when we've succeeded.

BROADCAST LIVE

One of the most powerful elements of social media for communications is the ability to broadcast live video from inside a classroom, board room, auditorium, or stadium—straight to the devices of your students' families and the community members who care about your schools. As live video tools have become accessible for social media managers, education leaders have explored ways to deliver value to their audiences.

Justin Elbert, a leader in the communications department in Klein ISD, outside Houston, Texas, has done just that. "Using live video has allowed our schools to directly reach parents during the school day with a relevant and timely peek into the daily life of their children," Elbert said. "Live video has removed the barrier that once existed between what parents think happens in the classroom and what actually happens— thoughtful and effective learning."

After experimenting with the new tool for small events (with a corresponding small audience), Elbert and his team discovered some tricks to increase engagement. "We found that people do not engage well with static live shots when the camera is on a tripod and doesn't engage with the activity. We changed to a 'roving camera' technique where we move the shot in and around the action, and we've seen engagement rates triple in return. Parents and our community want to feel like they are seeing 'behind the scenes.'"

Perhaps the most impressive live video effort at Klein came at a time of year when hundreds, if not thousands, of people are always paying attention—graduation. Elbert said the coordinated effort to provide a live stream of the high school graduation ceremonies at all four district high schools delivered unprecedented results. "We had almost two million impressions from all over the world," he said, "with thousands of comments. We used a streaming service—restream.io—to push our broadcast to Facebook, Twitter, and YouTube at the same time. The results far exceeded anything we expected."

An audience of millions may not be routine for most schools, but that hardly diminishes the power of live video for engaging families and the community. After all, the chance to bring parents inside the classroom is one that delivers value to even the smallest audience.

Ryan Jacobs, who teaches social studies at Eudora Middle School, used a series of Facebook live videos on a special day in his class. Jacobs and his students had been studying the role of abolitionist John Brown in Kansas history, and the unit ended as students reenacted the criminal trial held in Virginia to prosecute Brown for his involvement in the Harpers Ferry raid. "There were a number of people that could not attend our mock trial," Jacobs said. "It's something the kids had been working on for weeks and the one or two days that we had the culmination of this hard work, so it's really an amazing thing to be able to offer people that have other commitments the opportunity to see what their kids have been working so hard on. I truly believe it's a game changer for a classroom teacher."

Refer to chapter 7 for tips and considerations before ever clicking "go live" in your district accounts.

As a communications tool, social media can engage families and patrons—and tell the great stories of schools and districts—in ways that no other tool can. Applying the best practices of communications to any variety of social networks, in an intentional, targeted way, will yield results that far outweigh the risks of two-way communication that takes place publicly and online. There are times, however, when social media becomes a valuable outlet for sharing more difficult messages. Chapter 10 includes specific strategies to help education leaders manage even the most challenging situations on social media.

KEY IDEAS TO REMEMBER

- Effective communication on social media should follow the best practices of all kinds of communication: understanding the audience, having a specific goal, and selecting the best timing and channel that will ensure the message gets out.
- Messages on social media must be designed around what the audience needs or wants. Even administrative-driven information about business, policies, or procedures can be crafted to help hook the attention of key audience members.
- While not possible with every post, the very best social media content tells a story that prompts an emotional reaction from followers. Watch for opportunities to tell these stories on social networks, as often as possible.
- At its foundation, social media is a ready-made communications tool for schools and school districts. Remind parents and patrons that they need not even use the sites themselves to still access and receive updates and information from social media.
- Build and enrich your online community by involving your fans. Ask people to share your page, post to your page, and engage on your page. Posting community guidelines gives you a framework

to encourage appropriate participation and deal with occasional inappropriate use.

TEN

When Social Media Isn't Easy

Nasty Comments and Crisis Events

When leaders and educators are reluctant to embrace social media in schools, it's most often based on a fear of losing control. Empowering a large and diverse group of people to tell your school system's story — including employees, parents, patrons, and students — means giving up the ability to control what is being said. And this inevitably means that there occasionally will be people who complain, accuse, misinterpret, and air some dirty laundry in your online social media community. This can be, without question, a very uncomfortable part of the social media shift.

But remember that social media is simply a new tool for the communications that have always taken place. And just like the angry phone call, misleading letter to the editor, or agenda-driven individual at a town hall meeting, there are simple steps to take that will protect and improve your school's or district's public image and ensure that appropriate, constructive exchanges take place in your social media community — exchanges that can solve problems without letting emotions escalate any higher.

"If you're listening and paying attention, it isn't difficult to manage the responses to people who are angry," said Eudora consultant Ben Smith, who most often works with major corporations to provide expertise in managing a national brand on social media. "The most important thing is to treat someone online in the same way you would offline. If you ignore their comment or complaint, they're only going to get angrier. But if you acknowledge it and find ways to work toward a solution, good things will happen."

Indeed, as an education leader, you already know that the first step in solving a problem with someone who is angry or upset is to acknowledge the person's feelings and point of view. If you hear from a father who believes his child is being treated badly by a teacher, you do not simply turn a deaf ear and ignore him or his statements. Rather, you speak calmly, acknowledge his frustration, provide clarifying information if needed, and work toward a better mutual understanding.

Often, the angriest parents can become a great ally to someone who they feel took them seriously and treated them with respect. The same process works on social media—and because it happens in a public forum, it will even help build credibility for your school and district with all of your followers.

UGLY COMMENTS

Monitoring interactions with fans, followers, and group members is the job of each person who manages a social media account. Often, a space for leaving comments is the area most prone to negative interaction, whether on Facebook, blogs, YouTube, Instagram, or others.

As an education leader, the key to managing your responses to online comments—negative or otherwise—must be based on objective evaluation. Here are the questions to ask when you, or anyone in your school or district, discover a post about your school or school system that is negative or unbalanced:

1. Is the place where the comment is posted credible with strong viewership?
2. Was the post made on a site that is dedicated to bashing and degrading others?
3. Is the posting a rant, rage, joke, or satirical in nature?
4. Does the posting include misinformation or blatant lies?
5. Did a negative experience in our schools prompt the posting?

Depending on the answers to these questions, your next steps could include any of the following:

Monitor the Conversation Thread

Inserting yourself with a response is not always the place to start, no matter how great the temptation may be. Think of the old saying, "If a tree falls in the forest and nobody's there to hear it, does it make a sound?" In the case of social media, the answer is most usually *no*. For example, if someone with just ten Twitter followers tweets a random negative comment (*The teachers at George Washington Middle School sure are a bunch of idiots!*), it's unlikely to gain any steam—and engaging in the conversation could only add fuel to the fire.

Similarly, it's important to remember that the only people who will see what an individual posts to a Facebook page are those who visit the page directly (which is an extremely small percentage of your fans on any given day) and those who are both friends with the original poster *and also* fans of your page. Again, it's important to point out that this is most likely a very small fraction of the people who care about your school system.

Provide a Simple, Unemotional Response

Sometimes the best response to an emotional or angry post is simply to acknowledge the concern and clarify facts while neutralizing the emotion. Eudora leaders rarely respond to posts on news sites or public blogs maintained by people who are not employees in our schools, but they are committed to responding to comments and posts made on the social media sites managed by the schools or district. Certain jabs, complaints, and rants can undoubtedly trigger feelings of defensiveness, frustration, or anger in people who work and lead in the school district. But taking the time to respond unemotionally and directly can go a great distance in defusing an uncomfortable post.

Privately Contact the Original Commenter

Education leaders have access to contact information for students and employees and therefore should not hesitate to pick up the phone and make a personal call when needed. Approaching this conversation with a level head and desire to work together will be successful the vast majority of the time. It's important to stress to the commenter that you care about their problem, but that social media is not the best place to find a resolution. Often the commenter who clicked "post" in an emotional moment is ultimately grateful for the chance to resolve it privately with you. If a phone number isn't available, or if you don't have contact information for the commenter, a polite, unemotional email or direct message through the social media site also can be extremely effective.

The Eudora School District uses a flow chart to assess negative comments and posts that are made online. Not only is this chart an objective resource to help leaders make good decisions in moments when they may feel attacked, but it also helps everyone in the district know that there is a procedure in place to respond. This chart also comes in handy when leaders who are not directly involved, including school board members, question why a negative comment or post was handled in a particular way.

Solve Problems, But Don't Debate

Social media managers rarely know the answer to all the questions and complaints that appear on a social network, but it's still important to respond promptly and appropriately. When Eudora Elementary School was chosen to be featured in a documentary about bullying prevention efforts, this was cause for celebration. On the day when the camera crew was on-site, a photo was posted on the district's Facebook page of Principal Amy DeLaRosa being interviewed about the programs in her school that help identify and prevent bullying.

Despite the great number of likes, shares, and positive comments, over the next few hours, a small handful of parents made comments alluding to ongoing bullying problems affecting their children. In each case, official replies were promptly posted, reiterating the value the district places on working with parents and providing specific steps that could be taken for a resolution.

For example: "It takes all of us working together to make EES a safe and supportive place for students. Please contact Mrs. DeLaRosa or Mr. Heide in the office for support!" And in each case, the comment thread quickly ended. Although these types of comments felt uncomfortable in a celebratory post, they also provided district leaders the chance to publicly double down on their commitment to working with parents to help prevent bullying at school—so much so that other fans of the page even clicked the "like" button on the calm and supportive responses to those parents!

(The fact that these few parents posted their concerns also provided an important opportunity for principals to follow up directly, learn more about their experiences, and work privately on positive resolutions.)

Though rare, there are times when a negative post is intended to pick a fight or start a debate. Often the user making a post is too angry or emotional to seek a solution, and the intent of the post is to simply vent and seek an audience for his or her grievances. Again, in these cases the key is to maintain a level head, clarify the facts and/or the school's values, and avoid engaging in an argument.

A post from an angry father appeared on the Eudora School District Facebook page one morning, accusing the elementary school leaders of treating students unfairly and allowing one student to bully and sexually harass his daughter. The post did not name the alleged bully, so there was no breach of confidentiality. (If the student had been named, the post would have been immediately removed in accordance with the stated community guidelines.) After a short call to the principal to find out what might have caused this post, it was clear that this was a parent angry because he was dissatisfied with disciplinary consequences after a single incident involving his daughter and another student.

The district's first reply—to work with the school principals on a resolution and contact the superintendent if further support is needed—immediately triggered a response that the principals were the problem, and his daughter was at risk. The district's next reply was clear and simple: "Disciplinary matters cannot be resolved on this page and will not be discussed here. Please contact Superintendent Don Grosdidier to share your concerns."

The decision was made that the district would reply no further, and the father got the message. He did not choose to reengage, contacted the superintendent as suggested, and was able to communicate his frustrations in the proper channels.

If this type of exchange seems too risky for your school's or district's page, remember—the only people who saw this exchange in their news feed that day were people who were *both* Facebook friends with the father *and* fans of our page. The fact that it garnered no interaction from anyone other than the father who was posting indicates how insignificant these interactions truly are in terms of a district's overall public image.

NASTY POSTS ON OTHER PAGES

It's not uncommon for education leaders to find out about disparaging posts on the personal pages of parents or patrons, or in closed or private Facebook groups, dealing with anything ranging from taxes to a mix-up on a lunch line in the school cafeteria. Just as you monitor what's being printed in the newspaper or posted in the social media communities you manage, it's important to monitor what is being said about your district, schools, and employees in other places on the internet. By signing up for free notifications on Google Alerts and Mention.com, you can be made more aware of the conversations about your school system that are taking place in the digital world.

Intervening on any nondistrict social media accounts is rarely a positive strategy for education leaders to take when negative or misinformed posts are found. However, these can be golden opportunities to follow up privately with the individual—especially those parents with students currently enrolled in your school system—to find out more and connect them with the people who can help resolve their problem. Additionally, seeing that a parent has posted about a seemingly awful incident at school can be a chance for an administrator to investigate the concern internally to find out what really happened and potentially address any areas for improvement that may be revealed.

"Because we monitor mentions of our school on social media, we've had a number of opportunities to adjust and improve how we support students and families," EES principal DeLaRosa said. "Sometimes parents will air concerns or complaints about issues that aren't on our radar at all, and the alerts give me the ability to follow up with our teachers and staff and find positive resolutions."

STAND UP FOR EMPLOYEES

As mentioned in chapter 4, cyberbullying can occur in a single post, even if it's later deleted. The public nature of a message or photo shared on a social network means that a negative or false post about an employee has the potential to create a hostile work environment for that individual, even potentially hurting the victim's professional reputation.

For example, an accusation of a teacher inappropriately touching a student in a large metropolitan district was unsubstantiated by two prompt and independent investigations. But this didn't stop the parent of the student from threatening to post information about the teacher all over a personal Facebook page if the principal failed to make special arrangements for the student—arrangements that were simply impossible in this particular school.

"Knowing that a parent could go online and basically destroy this innocent teacher's career, and potentially this teacher's personal life, was definitely not okay," the principal shared. "Cyberbullying policies must include protections for the employees who are abused online by parents or students. Short of banning them from coming on our campus for games or activities, we can't take a lot away from parents who don't follow the policy. But they must know that we take this seriously and absolutely will not tolerate it."

SHARE BAD NEWS

Even in the most efficient and transparent school districts, mistakes are made. Sometimes they are embarrassing—a misprint on the school calendar or a sibling name accidentally provided on an awards list, for example. Other times, they are much more serious and upsetting to district employees and parents, alike—a sleeping child left on a bus, an employee arrested for a sex crime, or a failure to promptly communicate with parents and the community in a crisis, among others.

Social media is not a replacement for other communications channels, including the letters to parents, automated phone calls or email messages, and traditional media relations with reporters. However, social media does provide a level of immediacy and transparency that can be powerful in the right situation.

It was a winter afternoon when the offices in each school in Eudora received a call from the local police department, recommending a lockdown but providing little other detail. School leaders moved quickly to lock the buildings down but had virtually no idea why or for how long. Before long, the middle and high school principals both were notified that the threat had passed, but there was still concern about the elementary campus.

District crisis procedures include prompt parent notification during a lockdown, but the timing of the incident and lack of confirmed information made that difficult. "By the time we were able to reach someone at the police department and find out that the threat was a law enforcement operation now some distance from the school, there was less than a half hour left in the school day," said now-retired superintendent of schools Don Grosdidier. "We were concerned that sending a lockdown message so late in the day would create a lot of stress and chaos during dismissal, especially in an elementary building with more than eight hundred students."

But in the meantime, dozens of worried parents were posting their frustrations and concerns to their personal Facebook pages and to the pages of a local news blog. School dismissed normally on each campus, but within an hour after dismissal—and after sending an automated phone call and email message to district parents with an explanation of the afternoon's events—it became clear there was another opportunity to use Facebook to explain what happened and admit that the communication to parents during this crisis did not meet district leaders' own expectations.

Although this post far exceeded the target length for social media, it met the immediate needs of the community:

> From Superintendent Don Grosdidier:
> I want to thank our parents, staff and students for the patience they showed as we activated our crisis procedures this afternoon. On the advice of law enforcement, we had low-level lockdowns—meaning exterior doors were locked, and all activities were moved inside—beginning at approximately 1:30 p.m. at Eudora Elementary and from 1:30 to approximately 2:30 at EMS and EHS. This was a precautionary measure related to a law enforcement operation taking place approximately one mile northeast of EES.
>
> Our normal crisis procedures include notifying parents any time there is a lockdown; unfortunately, today's events unfolded in such a way that made that extremely difficult. It was very late in the school day before we fully understood the factors involved in the law enforcement operation in a way that we could have shared useful information with our families. At this point, we knew that dismissal would be taking place normally and did not want to create any further confusion or concern.
>
> As always, student safety is our top priority, and we will continue to strive for the most effective operations in our schools and the most timely and transparent communications with our families in times of crisis."

Unsurprisingly, comments began piling up as soon as the message was posted. The most surprising and gratifying result, however, was the number of likes and comments that were posted, thanking district leaders for their efforts. For every challenging comment—*It was stressful not to get a call and hope [sic] you can get these procedures down in the future!*—came multiple messages of acknowledgment and thanks. As the comments rolled in, the tone even shifted into gratitude that parents were not notified earlier! For example:

> I appreciated the phone call when it came. I was a little miffed that I didn't get a phone call at the time it happened, until my daughter told me it was probably a good thing the call didn't come, because I probably would have ended up going to the school and getting in the way . . . she was right. I appreciate the safety of my kids being the number one concern of the administration and my need to be "in the know" was put further down on the list of priorities. Although I would like to be in control of every minute of my children's lives, I have to trust the school district to keep them safe for me. I think today showed that the district is capable of doing that. Well done.

Reviewing these kinds of insightful (and incredibly generous) comments demonstrates that, more than anything, parents appreciate having their fears and frustrations acknowledged. It's important here to note that Grosdidier did not apologize for anything—there was nothing to apologize for, as the delayed communication was forced by circumstance, not by negligence or failure. Nor did he place the blame on an imperfect communication loop with the police department that afternoon—doing that would not have solved anything and only would have damaged efforts to improve communications in the future.

Grosdidier simply explained some of the circumstances that led to the slow notification and acknowledged that it was a worrisome afternoon for many parents. Although this is just one example of using social media to deliver uncomfortable messages, it is an illustration of the kind of supportive community that can be built when there is a genuine commitment on the part of education leaders to treat social media audiences with the highest levels of kindness and respect.

Most certainly, the primary content goal of social media use by schools and districts should be celebrating the great things happening every day. But using this channel to mindfully communicate the occasional piece of high-stakes bad news can have a major positive effect on the support and loyalty you receive from your fans and followers.

In *no way* is social media the right avenue for every piece of bad news, and it's important to maintain a proper balance so that those "bad news" messages catch the attention of your audience as different from your typical content. But there definitely are times when using a well-engaged social media account for communicating negative news gets the information out quickly, addresses the critics head-on, and ultimately builds enormous support for your school and district.

USE THE POWER OF SOCIAL

Even schools in the most supportive communities still must engage in policies, decisions, and outcomes that can be upsetting to people—and it's perfectly natural to be anxious when you are preparing to share information that you know will be controversial. Social media, however, includes unique features that can make your job easier, even when the message is difficult.

It's Fast

It's true that bad news travels fast, and there are few modes faster than social media to get a message to a lot of people. Consider the analogy of ripping off a bandage—in most cases, it's best to do it all at once because it may sting more, but the pain will be shorter. Most importantly, posting your message on social media will also ensure that *your story*—the angle, facts, and tone you want to share—is out there first.

Fans Are Passionate

When there is bad news to share, it's wise to anticipate that many of the comments from the public will be challenging or critical. But do not underestimate the passion and loyalty of your fans—the parents, students, alumni, patrons, and employees who often speak in your defense. When threads of comments get heated, it's common to see fans taking the initiative to jump in and cool things down.

People Want to Share

Social media is all about sharing, so take advantage. Following the construction of a new district stadium in Eudora, district leaders worked with a demolition crew to remove the press box and bleachers from the old, beloved football field, as they had become public safety hazards. Since this would require closing the public track for a few days—during Homecoming Week, no less—an announcement was made on the district's Facebook page. Unsurprisingly, this message evoked a number of comments from people who were still upset that the old stadium would be going away.

Turning this news around, a request was made on the Facebook page for people to share all their best memories of the old field and stadium. Without hesitation, these same commenters started posting memories of their own high school days. Instead of reasons for anger, their nostalgia was turned into positive connections and reflections.

BE PREPARED

As with all areas of crisis management, planning how and when to use social media in the district's communications response is key to swift, effective execution when the stakes are high. Managers of school and district social media accounts should take the time to prepare short, targeted messages that can be shared over social networks in a wide variety of crisis events. Writing these messages in advance will save precious time when a crisis strikes, ensuring that your story will get out quickly and clearly.

Given the nature of social media, it will also provide shareable content so that your fans and followers—and likely media outlets—can share your statement and actually help tell your story. Generic messages that can be quickly tailored by plugging in a few details should be written for school lockdown, school shooting, student suicide, medical emergency, natural disaster, bus accident, communicable disease, and any other events that might require the activation of your school or district crisis plan.

It's also important to recognize that there are sometimes events that happen outside of your school or community that have a serious effect on your students, employees, and parents. Whether a tragic school shooting, dramatic child abduction, devastating tornado, or some other major news event, social media can be a powerful tool to ensure that your audiences feel connected and supported.

Following the massacre at Sandy Hook Elementary in 2012, parent-friendly resources were collected and posted on the Eudora district website to help parents and families manage the fears and emotions that come when there is tragedy in the news. This web page now allows school and district leaders to easily share these resources—on social media, through parent communications, or with individual families—whenever support is needed.

Education leaders who embrace the social media shift in their schools will soon find that social media brings with it countless opportunities and advantages. And it is absolutely certain that the difficult encounters—crisis communications, angry complaints, rumors, misinformation and different sorts of bad news—are quickly offset by the benefits of building and enjoying a supportive, engaged community of fans and followers who are passionate about your schools.

KEY IDEAS TO REMEMBER

- It's perfectly normal to be afraid of angry people making negative comments or posts on social media. But handling the conversation with an angry parent or patron is something that education leaders do every day—and the same strategies work in the digital world to de-escalate emotions and find solutions to problems.

- There are specific factors to consider before determining how to handle an angry post. A formal process or flow chart that is shared among all employees can help everyone understand how to make good, sound decisions when emotions run high.
- Your employees must be protected from attacks on social media, which—even if completely untrue—can create lasting damage for a career and personal life. Policies and procedures empower administrators to handle these attacks or cyberbullying incidents when they take place.
- Social media can be a powerful place to share bad news. If done intentionally and strategically, this type of digital messaging will not only get the message out, but also help build credibility and loyalty over time among followers and fans.
- Social media communications should be part of the emergency planning done in every school and district. Scripting out sample messages before a crisis hits will give district leaders a major advantage and help ensure in the fast-paced digital world that you are the first to tell your story.

Conclusion

Social media is now. And social networks are constantly changing and evolving—often at a pace that can both boggle and bewilder. Not unlike my experience writing the first edition of this book in 2014, I once again feel a bit like I am creating a time capsule. Seeing the growth since the first edition—the technology and tools, the expectations, and the sheer number of teachers, leaders, and districts using social media—it's clear that any book like this is doomed to looking outdated and out of style to a reader a few short years from now.

At the rate that the digital world changes, it would be foolish and shortsighted to outline the latest tools and trends. Those topics are better suited to magazines and blogs, where readers can learn the latest strategies to take the greatest advantage of current online behavior trends, site settings, and algorithms.

By the time you're reading this book, I am certain that the digital landscape will have changed significantly from this day I'm writing. The numerous examples and stories provided in this book should be understood as illustrations used to paint the picture of just how powerful social media can be for student learning and growth—and how important it is for teachers to try new ways to use social media tools to engage their students in the learning process.

Ultimately, the power of social media in education is much less about *how* it is used—and much more about the fact *that* it is used. After all, the specific uses of social media will look different as the tools we know today change and new ones emerge. But what will not change is the importance of using these tools to engage our learning community and—ultimately—do our work better.

But I'm also certain that the opportunities for teaching and learning on social media will only continue to grow and evolve, making these tools truly indispensable to the twenty-first-century school system—from students, to staff members, to the communities that surround us. Social media is—and always will be—now.

About the Author

Kristin Magette, APR, is an award-winning public relations professional and advocate for service, strategic communications, and collaboration. A well-known leader in school public relations and co-moderator of #k12PRchat, she also is a proud lifelong Kansan who always makes time for family, friends, big laughs, and great food.